ITALIA

ITALIA

The Art of Living Italian Style

EDMUND HOWARD
PHOTOGRAPHY BY OLIVER BENN

A THOMAS DUNNE BOOK

ST MARTIN'S PRESS ✦ NEW YORK

Pour Cécile avec laquelle Italia m'est toujours parue plus belle encore.

Text © The Hon. Edmund Howard 1996
Photographs © Oliver Benn 1996

The Hon. Edmund Howard has asserted his moral right to be identified as the author of this book in accordance with the Copyright, Design and Patents Act 1988.

First published in Great Britain in 1996

First U.S. Edition: 1997

10 9 8 7 6 5 4 3 2 1

A Thomas Dunne Book. An imprint of St. Martin's Press.

A CIP catalog entry for this book is available from the Library of Congress.

ISBN 0–312–14811–9

Designed by Lisa Tai
Edited by Colin Grant

Printed and bound in Italy

Page One: The garden of the Villa Rufolo, Ravello, Campania.
Page Two-Three: Asolo, Veneto.
Opposite: The Neptune fountain in the Piazza Navona, Rome.

AUTHOR'S ACKNOWLEDGEMENTS
Many members of my family have helped me with the typing and correcting of drafts for the texts which accompany the magnificent photographs in this book. I am most grateful to Esme and Diane, John and Gloria, Tonino and Bridget, my sons and their wives; and to my brother Francis, my grand-daughter-in-law Emma and my friend John Vernon for much valuable assistance in England. From Italy I received very helpful information through another great friend Vera Larsimont-Pergameni Saija in Turin. And my special thanks are due to the copyeditor of this book, Colin Grant, who with great patience and unfailing skill gave my sometimes wayward and capricious text an appearance of order and lucidity.

PHOTOGRAPHER'S ACKNOWLEDGEMENTS
I am particularly grateful to Gaia Neubert-Tacconi, of the Association of Italian Historic Houses, for her introductions, advice and assistance during the preparation of this book; and to Colin Grant for his valuable editorial contribution. The following, who are listed in alphabetical order, have also been especially helpful: Rossella Barletta, Simon and Julia Blunt, Jacopo Cicogna-Mozzoni, David Ellero, Professor Nicola Galante, Professor Bernard Hickey, Esme and Diane Howard, Contessa Cettina Lanzara, Patricia Liani, Ian Lowe, Francesca Martirani, Laura Marzano, Lorenza de' Medici Stucchi, Polizia Municipale of Alberobello, Ron Radley and Marchese Rosselli Del Turco.

CONTENTS

INTRODUCTION

'*Che bello!*' and '*O bella!*' are exclamations which may be heard at any moment of the day or night, in any place all over Italy from men, women and children of every description. These expressions are an automatic reaction to any pleasurable experience. They indicate in a very natural and spontaneous way the intimate relationship in Italian sensibility between beauty and happiness. And I think it is arguable that the output of beauty through the ages has been higher in Italy, in proportion to the size of the country, than in any other region of the world.

In some respects the Italians have been fortunate. They were born in a country of quite extraordinary beauty and diversity. They have also had the advantage of seeing a high standard of beauty among their fellow human beings, and they have shown a touching sensibility to the beauty of their women as the story of a Genoese girl, Simonetta Cattaneo, demonstrates. She grew up in Piombino, where her parents lived in exile, and turned out to be an exceedingly beautiful girl, who at the age of fourteen was married to Marco Vespucci, a young member of a well-known family of Florentine merchants. The Vespucci mansion in Florence was the resort of some outstanding painters, among them Domenico Ghirlandaio and Sandro Botticelli. This was the time when Lorenzo de' Medici had succeeded his father as the ruler of Florence. He and his younger brother, Giuliano, were fond of arranging spectacular entertainments and in 1475, during one of these events, Simonetta was crowned the Queen of Beauty. In the tournament Giuliano's standard was painted by Botticelli. It represented Simonetta as Pallas Athena in a field of flowers. On 26 April 1476, however, soon after being crowned Queen

of Beauty, Simonetta died from consumption at the age of twenty-three; three years later Giuliano was assassinated in the cathedral of Florence by enemies of the Medici.

When Simonetta was buried in the church of Ognissanti the whole of Florence turned out to see the vision of her beauty as they carried her to the tomb in an open coffin: artists and friends, humanists and poets, the entire Vespucci family,

ABOVE: *The Via Monte d'Oro in Martina Franca, Apulia.*

RIGHT: *Part of the Salone Centrale in the Palazzina di Caccia di Stupinigi, Piedmont.*

OVERPAGE: *Canal and houses in the Fondamenta Cavanella, Burano, an island in the Venetian lagoon.*

the civic authorities, the clergy and a host of friends accompanied the bier. All along the way from balconies and windows the people looked down to see Simonetta for the last time. Even after the burial there were artists who could not forget her beauty. Leonardo da Vinci went home and drew a portrait of her. Many years later Piero di Cosimo remembered seeing the procession when he was only fourteen and painted from memory a famous portrait now in the Museum of Chantilly in France. Of the remembered representations of Simonetta, the most famous are those in two paintings by Sandro Botticelli in the Uffizzi Gallery in Florence: *Primavera*, or 'Spring' (*c*.1478), and the somewhat later *Birth of Venus*, when the graceful nude figure of Venus inspired by Simonetta balances lightly on a large sea shell blown ashore by a puffing Zephyr.

The feeling for beauty which drew the people of Florence to witness the passing of Simonetta is perhaps innate. It has certainly been a feature of Italian life and activity in all ages. Even in our modern age of mass production, prefabrication and industrial output we can still observe a distinct and highly elegant Italian style emerging in the manufacture of all kinds of goods in Italy and in a large range of building work. We see it in clothes and footwear, in household furniture and consumer durables, in cars and ships. It also shows itself in larger projects, from motorways to railway stations, from sporting arenas to power stations, and in the creation of new villas and gardens. By combining beauty with comfort and liveliness, the Italians are able to provide the joy in life which their conquerors in the past, no less than their friends and visitors at all times, have found unfailingly irresistible.

TOWNS AND LANDSCAPES

ABOVE: *The medieval village of Baiardo stands on a spur of the maritime alps north of San Remo, surrounded by vineyards and olive groves.*

LEFT: *View over Lucca looking south from the tower of the Palazzo Guinigi, showing characteristic terracotta-tiled roofs, Romanesque campaniles and the surrounding hills.*

TOWNS AND LANDSCAPES

The traveller who wishes to make the most dramatic possible entry into Italy, compatible with comfort, would be well advised to take his car through the Mont Blanc tunnel to emerge at the head of the Valle d'Aosta surrounded by the glaciers, pinnacled ridges and mighty rock faces of the south side of the highest mountain in the Alps. This great chain of mountains, covering the shoulders of Italy from Ventimiglia to Trieste, seemingly a mighty bulwark against foreign foes, did not prevent Italy

LEFT: *The cloister of the medieval church of Sant' Orso, Aosta, was founded by Saint Anslem (d.1109). Part of it was built in the twelfth century, while the arches and vaulted ceiling date from the fifteenth.*

BELOW LEFT: *A typical small town in the Aosta valley, surrounded by apple orchards and vineyards. Mont Blanc rises at the head of the valley and the tunnel through it is the main access to Italy by road from the north-west.*

from being regularly invaded by barbarians.

The tossing waters of the glacier-fed Dora Baltea river lead south-eastward along the rapidly falling and gradually widening valley past small and picturesque Alpine villages, until you reach the first town of any size, Aosta, which like so many towns in Italy was a Roman foundation. Set in a wide plain among high mountains, it still retains a Roman gateway and part of its Roman walls as well as the ruins of a forum and a theatre. The remaining walls disclose the outline of a typical Roman colonial town, a rectangle with the walls and a gateway on each side built around a double axis, that going east–west called the *decumanus* and that going north–south, the *cardo*, with the forum at the central intersection. Aosta also contains fine specimens of Romanesque and Gothic architecture in the cathedral and the church of San Orso, the latter founded by Aosta's most distinguished citizen, St Anselm, who became Archbishop of Canterbury in 1093.

Continuing down the 100-kilometre (60-mile)-long valley, we pass a number of attractive villages and a succession of imposing castles – Issogne, Fénis and Verrès among them. These were built in the fourteenth and fifteenth centuries by members of the Challant family who were the viscounts of the valley. After emerging from its accompaniment of high-flanking mountains at the valley's end, the Dora Baltea continues on a more placid course across the western end of the Po plain, joining Italy's longest river about 40 kilometres (25 miles) east of Turin.

RIGHT: *View from the Scaliger bridge, Verona, over the fast-flowing River Adige as it sweeps past the town's main fortification, the Castelvecchio, seen on the right.*

BELOW: *The picturesque medieval town of Porlezza lies at the foot of the Alps on the north-east side of Lake Lugano.*

Palladian details in Vicenza – the first-floor loggia of the Basilica designed by Palladio but only completed after his death, and on the right a corner of his Loggia del Capitanato (1571).

The nearby city of Vicenza is of particular interest to lovers of Palladian architecture. Palladio was educated there from the age of thirteen and a number of his best buildings were erected there.

Like the small towns round the lakes, those in the foothills of the Alps to the north of Venice have also attracted many foreign admirers and Asolo has been a special favourite for generations of English people. Among them are the poet Robert Browning – his 'drama' *Pippa Passes* was set in and around Asolo – and the remarkable explorer and writer Freya Stark. Asolo is a partly medieval city with a number of Gothic houses but also some Renaissance buildings. About halfway between Vicenza and Venice stands the ancient city of Padua famed for its fine basilica dedicated to St Anthony, the Portuguese friar who became a celebrated preacher there in the thirteenth

Almost directly northward across the Po plain among the foothills of the Alps is the first of the Italian lakes, the small and rather sombre Lake Orta. This marks the beginning of the Italian Lake District, an area greatly renowned for its scenic beauty. Next to Lake Orta is the large, bright Lake Maggiore, with the gorgeous Baroque villa and gardens of the Borromeo family on Isola Bella. Further east lies the three-pronged, and partly Swiss, Lake Lugano. Here at the northern end of the main arm of the lake is the strikingly picturesque little town of Porlezza. With its tall church tower and white houses with red roofs against the green background of the tree-covered

Alpine foothills beyond the blue water, this is a typical Italian lakeland setting. Moving east, one reaches Lake Como, directly to the north of Milan. Its predominant colour is green with a number of attractive little towns and beautiful villas along its shores.

The last in line is the greatest, and to my mind the most beautiful, of all these lakes, Lake Garda, usually of a deep blue colour. Near its southern end on the banks of the River Adige stands the splendid city of Verona, founded in 89 BC and like Aosta one of the Roman colonial cities. It controlled access to the Brenner pass into Austria and remained for most of its history a fortress city.

The Via Robert Browning in Asolo, which was twice visited by the poet in 1838 and again in 1889 when he stayed in this street for two months shortly before his death in Venice.

A typical undulating landscape near Asolo in the foothills of the Alps.

century. Padua is also renowned for its university which was founded in 1222. But perhaps its most remarkable asset is the Scrovegni chapel with Giotto's frescoes (1303–5), which revolutionised the art of painting in Italy. Among its amenities Padua has the largest piazza in Italy, the Prato della Valle, with a combination of water and statuary so dear to the Italians.

Moving to the sea, we can make our entry into one of Italy's major cities, Venice. Opinions about it have differed violently, but whatever else one may say there is no disputing that it is entirely unique. Surrounded by a lagoon, it is infiltrated by water throughout its length and breadth, and built

for the most part over millions of wooden piles sunk vertically into the mud so as to bear the weight of the finest cluster of palaces and churches anywhere assembled in so small a space. And its history is no less extraordinary than its buildings.

Venice is one of four remarkable Italian cities whose wealth depended on the sea. They were known as maritime republics and accumulated their wealth and power through the skills and enterprise of their merchants. The Venetians, originally refugees from the mainland at the time

of the barbarian invasions from the sixth to the tenth centuries, were protected and assisted by the Byzantine emperors. Genoa at the north-western end of the peninsula and Pisa in Tuscany both developed as great maritime powers in the eleventh century, and Amalfi, south of Naples, somewhat earlier. Their seagoing capability was greatly stimulated by the need to react against the swift expansion of Islamic power in the eighth to the tenth centuries and the raids of Arab fleets or pirate flotillas on European and Italian shores. Venice's naval capabilities are strikingly demonstrated in a record for the year 1423: her navy numbered 300 warships and her merchant

The Prato della Valle in Padua, perhaps the largest public square in Italy, was designed by Andrea Memmo in 1775. The central feature is an elliptical island enclosed by a canal, on each side of which runs a parapet supporting a succession of large eighteenth-century statues on high pedestals. These represent local notables, and one is by Antonio Canova.

ABOVE: *Over the entrance arch of the Venice Arsenal is an aedicule enclosing a finely carved, winged lion of St Mark, the symbol of Venice and its patron saint.*

LEFT: *A medium-sized palace in the Venetian-Gothic style of the fifteenth century on the Grand Canal in Venice. This is the main thoroughfare of the city flanked by over a hundred fine palaces, large and small, in a variety of styles.*

OPPOSITE: *The Arsenal entrance (1460), in the form of a triumphal arch, is one of the earliest Renaissance works in Venice. Attributed to Antonio Gambello of Venice (d.1479), it is flanked by pairs of free-standing fluted columns carrying eleventh-century Veneto-Byzantine capitals. The lion on the right, one of several keeping guard around the entrance, was taken from Athens.*

OVERPAGE: *The Grand Canal, Venice, from the Accademia bridge, showing a number of famous palaces in different styles. Towards the centre of the left bank there is the fifteenth-century Gothic Palazzo Loredan, while at the end of the left bank is one of the most grandiose palaces in Venice, the Palazzo Rezzonico, a Baroque masterpiece by Baldasarre Longhena, completed by Giorgio Massari (c.1667-1746) and now a museum.*

navy 3,000 cargo vessels. During a visit by King Henry III of France a warship was built, rigged, armed and launched from the Arsenal in a single day.

The maritime republics were immensely successful in developing trade with the eastern Mediterranean, satisfying the Europeans' craving for pepper and spices to improve the flavours of their food and for silks to improve the homespun appearance of their clothes, while the Orientals' need for warmth in a climate of hot days and cold nights, and for arms to wage war against their enemies, including the European Christians, was equally catered for without discrimination by shipments of wool, iron and weapons. The wealth generated among the great merchant families both in Venice and Genoa made possible the construction in both cities of grand palaces, villas and monuments. The Grand Canal in Venice and the Via Garibaldi in Genoa show a concentration of palaces not equalled in any other European cities.

What we have seen so far may lead us to the conclusion that for sustained beauty and diversity Italian landscapes, within the small area they occupy, cannot be bettered. It must be admitted, however, that on the Adriatic coastline of Italy there are places where Nature appears to have flagged. It is quite otherwise if we move over to the Gulf of Genoa. The journey leads across the Po plain, the richest and most extensive agricultural area in Italy, where a seemingly unending succession of fruit orchards, rice-fields, water-meadows, vines festooned over willow, elm and poplar trees, mulberry trees and pastures, fills you with a somewhat stifling satisfaction. The inhabitants of the Po Valley are, however, notoriously heavy eaters and all the produce is put to good use.

The best way to reach Genoa is on the highway from Milan and there, near the end of the journey early in the year, you may experience one of Italy's

LEFT: *A display of salami and other meats at a delicatessen shop, including salami cinghiali (boar), prosciutto cinghiali, capocolli and lonze.*

LEFT: *Fruit and vegetables play a large part in the Italian diet and are often bought from a local market, such as here in the Piazza Campo dei Fiori, Rome.*

climatic surprises. For on entering the Giovi tunnel to go through the last crest of the Apennines before reaching the sea, you leave fog and snow and winter behind you to emerge on the other side in the spring sunshine of the riviera.

To the west of Genoa is the Riviera di Ponente, a coastline now somewhat spoiled by over-building but which retains pockets of outstanding beauty like the Hanbury Gardens at La Mortola. There are also some attractive medieval villages in the valleys behind the coast, nestling among olive orchards on the hillsides, like Apricale and Baiardo near San Remo. To the east of Genoa the Riviera di Levante, with its alternating beaches, coves and rocky headlands where the cliffs fall sheer to the sea, is one of the most impressive coastal stretches in Italy. Along this coast are highly picturesque and colourful fishing villages like Portofino and charming seaside towns like Rapallo. In the former, Montague Yeats-Brown, when consul in Genoa, made a home in the castle, and the aristocratic statesman Lord Carnarvon and the renowned actor Rex Harrison built villas. In Rapallo Max Beerbohm found a restful haven. Further south the Cinque Terre, five small towns in the recesses of the cliff-girdled shore, are still justifiably renowned. Vernazza and Corniglia with their brightly coloured houses are particularly beautiful.

A short way beyond the deep indented Gulf of La Spezia the mountains recede from the sea making way for a gradually widening coastal plain with the range of the sharply outlined Apuanian Alps rising behind it. At the lower end of the coastal plain is Pisa astride the River Arno and to the north-west is Lucca, both cities which contain some of the best Tuscan Romanesque architecture in Italy. The Arno valley leads us to Florence surrounded by hills, the inheritor of the Etruscan genius and birthplace of the Renaissance, though its art treasures cover the whole range of Italian art. The artistic pre-eminence of nearly all the Tuscan cities began in the Middle Ages when they were independent Communes and vied with one another to build the most impressive town halls

LEFT: *A restaurant in Milan, showing some typical north Italian dishes, including Frittate Ripiene, Osso Buco, Torta Salata and Peperoni Ripieni.*

LEFT: *Corniglia, one of the Cinque Terre of the eastern riviera of Liguria, famous for their beauty and their wine. The brightly painted houses are set on steep slopes over vineyards spread out on terraces above the cliffs.*

OVERPAGE: *The fishing village of Portofino on the eastern riviera of Liguria, with its charming waterfront piazza and small, well-sheltered port, was for long a magnet for wealthy English Italophiles who have been replaced by Italian industrialists. The main features of this former possession of the Genoese Republic, whose patron saint was St George, are the castle and church of San Giorgio.*

and cathedrals.

The landscapes around Florence, Lucca and Siena have become familiar to generations of English and American travellers. The clear but gentle light, and the inviting undulations of the hills covered by vineyards and olive trees, with sometimes a single cypress thrusting up skyward, sometimes an avenue of these notable trees mounting a hillside to a cleverly sited villa or cemetery, all beget memories of Tuscany that constantly recur. The Tuscan farmer from his simple farmhouse (or *casa colonica*) has over the centuries worked his plot of land with such an understanding of the needs of nature as well as those of his family that large areas of the

countryside have the look of a garden extended over hill and dale.

No less fascinating than the larger towns are some of the small towns of Tuscany like San Gimignano 'of the beautiful towers'. It was a common practice of the leading families in the Italian cities of the Middle Ages to have fortified town houses, a component of which was a tall tower. The taller the tower the easier it was to hurl missiles at your neighbour when the fighting started. Towers grew to unimaginable heights and fighting from towers became more and more dangerous until in most towns laws were passed limiting their height or abolishing them altogether. In San Gimignano thirteen towers survive out of a

reputed seventy-seven.

South of Florence on the way to Rome there is Siena, another Tuscan city of striking beauty. Like Florence it has a notable history much of which consisted of efforts to shake off Florentine supremacy after 1165 when it became independent. It is famous for its black and white marble Gothic cathedral completed in 1215, its town hall with a soaring tower (1310) and some fine palaces and painters. Its central sloping piazza, the Campo, is the scene each year of the most colourful and alarming of horse races, the Palio.

Moving east towards the head-waters of the Arno River brings you to another large town,

Arezzo, an Etruscan then a Roman city, which became a Commune with its own consuls in 1098. The church of San Francesco contains some of the finest work of Piero della Francesca, one of Italy's greatest painters, and a remarkable stained–glass window by Guillaume de Marseille. The Piazza Grande is surrounded by fine buildings.

Somewhat further to the north-east is the astonishing small city of Urbino dwarfed by its vast ducal palace, a masterpiece of Renaissance art built between 1465 and 1472 by a Dalmatian architect, Luciano Laurana, for Federico da Montefeltro, a famous soldier and scholar. Almost due south of Urbino, in the inland region of

Florence from the south, showing on the right Brunelleschi's superb cathedral dome (1439), to the left Giotto's famous campanile (1334-43) and further to the left the fine medieval tower of the town hall (Palazzo Vecchio) attributed to Arnolfo di Cambio (1310).

Umbria with its constellation of beautiful hill-towns above silvery green valleys, each with its own entrancing prospects, there is one town with a rare reputation among Italian cities for a rare quality, that of sanctity. This is of course Assisi. The great series of frescoes by Giotto about the life of St Francis in the basilica dedicated to him displays a mingling of piety and beauty which is

symbolic of the whole place. The town is largely medieval, built of stone houses with rough-cast walls and dressed stone only around doorways and windows. Another town in the neighbouring region of the Marches, Ascoli Piceno, displays a varied but harmonious collection of styles. Its Roman origin is indicated by a Roman bridge, its medieval democracy by the town hall (except for the Baroque façade) and the thirteenth-century Palace of the People, and its Renaissance inclinations by parts of the main church, while the Neoclassical mood is exhibited in the theatre and a nod to Art Nouveau is provided in one of the popular cafés.

Due south of Ascoli Piceno is the mountainous region of the Abbruzzi where the Gran Sasso d'Italia, the highest peak of the Apennines, rises to 2670 metres (8750 feet). Not far south of this is the National Park of the Abruzzi, 40,145 hectares (155 square miles) in area, a forest and mountain habitat of brown bears, wolves and wild cats, of the golden eagle and the great eagle owl. The capital of this region is the university town of L'Aquila, comparatively recent in origin, having been founded in 1240 by the Emperor Frederick II. Going west towards the Tyrrhenian coastal area into the heartland of the Etruscan country you find the picturesque Lake Bracciano, from the springs of which the Emperor Trajan's aqueduct, which supplied northern areas of Rome, was fed. This source and other supplies from the north were combined by Pope Paul V to feed his large Fontana Paola, created in 1612 by the architects Giovanni Fontana and Flaminio Ponzio in the form of a triumphal arch. It was only completed in 1690 by Carlo Fontana for Pope Alexander VIII. The view of Rome from the piazza in front of the fountain is one of the best, in which the colour of the city's buildings can be clearly observed, including the white glare of the monument of King Victor Emmanuel II.

Around Rome lies the Campagna Romana, an undulating plain of open and at times rather arid country of faded grassland sprinkled here and there with clumps of reeds, asphodels and oleander bushes, with a scattering of farmhouses looking like fortresses and Roman monuments like the Claudian aqueduct or the tomb of Cecilia Metella. It was these monuments in their solitary grandeur, together with the contour of hills, which inspired famous artists like Poussin, Claude and Corot to paint the Campagna so contentedly and perhaps induced Lord Chesterfield in the 1840s to found the Roman hunt.

To the south-east of Rome the Alban hills were the setting for Alba Longa, the capital of the

LEFT: A cluster of towers in San Gimignano, Tuscany. Most were built in the twelfth and thirteenth centuries as part of a palazzo, and were used as vantage points for carrying on feuds.

BELOW: The famous towers of San Gimignano can be seen from afar. The surrounding vineyards produce the famed Vernaccia wine.

Alban League, of which Rome was originally a colony. They stand at the northern end of what was the Pontine Marsh, a coastal plain and a rich reservoir of alluvial soil which emperors and popes, and finally Mussolini, tried to free from the bane of malaria. It was the Americans who succeeded in this after World War II. Since then the marsh has been transformed into an area of intensive cultivation and later of industry so that its wild beauty has been largely destroyed. But around its edges some marvels still survive – the gardens at Ninfa, the castle and medieval town of Sermoneta and at the southern end of the plain the mythological mountain of Circe.

ABOVE: *The Piazza Grande in Arezzo, Tuscany, with the arcaded apse of the twelfth-century Romanesque church of Pieve di Santa Maria on the left, the law courts in the middle and the mixed Gothic and Renaissance façade of the Palazetto della Fraternità dei Laici under the large sixteenth-century bell tower on the right.*

LEFT: *Siena's central square, the Campo, with the soaring tower of the Gothic Palazzo Pubblico, or town hall (1297-1310), on the right. The piazza owes its rounded shape to its construction on the site of a Roman forum.*

RIGHT: *Urbino in the Marche region became an important centre of culture under Federico da Montefeltro who ruled it from 1444 to 1482. He employed Luciano Laurana from Dalmatia as the main architect for his immense ducal palace (1465-72), which dominates the town, and then filled it with outstanding works of art.*

ABOVE: *The small medieval town of Assisi, Umbria, with the famous shrine and basilica of St Francis, reclines on a spur of a hill surrounded by olive groves. Narrow streets of grey and russet stone rise towards a castle at the top.*

LEFT: *A gateway leading into the castle at Sermoneta south of Rome. A fief of the ancient Roman family of the Caetani, this massive castle was originally built in the thirteenth century and re-fortified in the sixteenth by Antonio Sangallo the Elder (d.1539).*

OPPOSITE: *The Piazza del Popolo, Ascoli Piceno, in the Marche region. On the left is the thirteenth-century town hall with a fine portal by Cola dell' Amatrice (1489-1559). Opposite is an arcaded Renaissance building (1507-9) attributed to Bernardo di Pietro da Carona, and in the background is the late Gothic church of San Francesco (1258-1461).*

On the way to Naples the coastline is varied and shapely with mountain spurs thrusting into the sea and re-entrants forming gulfs until another wide plain is reached such as the Campania of Naples, which was so fertile that it was known to the Romans as Campania Felix. The Bay of Naples is a byword for beauty, with Vesuvius as the backdrop, the sea and the perfect arc of the bay in the foreground and the city lining the waterfront in the middle. This was the place where 'seeing the Mediterranean', the grand object of travel as Dr Johnson defined it, was finally fulfilled for the English traveller on the Grand Tour.

The region of Campania stretches from the Gulf of Gaeta in the north to the Gulf of Policastro in the south. Just below the Sorrento peninsula we find a stretch of rocky coastline which is even more exciting than that of the Cinque Terre in Liguria. The road, which is often carved out of the cliff-side, ranges from 18 to 180 metres (60–600 feet) above sea level, rising and falling at the foot of towering crags and mountains 900 to 1200 metres (3000–4000 feet) high. Below the peaks there are plateaus from which the bare rock precipices fall vertically into the sea. This cincture of cliffs is broken every now and then by a deep ravine, and where the gap is wide enough, a sandy beach appears. In this dramatic setting are to be found the small town of Positano set on descending terraces overhanging the sea; Amalfi, once the capital of the important maritime republic of that name around a small bay with a beach; and Ravello, a satellite of Amalfi, which gained its independence in 1086. It clings to a spur of the mountain at about 300 metres (1000 feet) above the sea with wonderful views of the coast from the Villa Rufolo, once inhabited in 1156 by the only English pope, Nicholas Breakspeare, who became Hadrian VI. These towns, in addition to their striking situation, are endowed with churches and palaces which are masterpieces in the

Lombard-Norman and Saracenic-Norman styles.

There is nothing on the eastern coast of Italy to match the dramatic beauty of the southern shore of the Sorrentine peninsula. But in the region of Apulia there are landscapes of great beauty and an assembly of fine buildings of different styles in towns which until fairly recently were rarely visited by foreigners and can even now imbue the enterprising tourist with the thrill of discovery. At the north end of the region the vast tableland known as the Tavoliere della Puglia was one of the granaries of the Roman Empire. For centuries the Tavoliere was given over to pasture, and immense flocks of sheep and goats were herded into the mountains each year during the hot months, forming wide tracks across the countryside called *tratturi*.

The coastline of Apulia is a long and fairly level stretch of low rocks interspersed with little coves and occasional beaches. Along or near the shore is a chain of small towns with one big city, Bari, which is the capital. These cities are noted for their architecture especially in the very fine Norman-built churches. In an upland region of the province of Bari called Le Murge, in and around the three delightful towns of Alberobello,

ABOVE: *View of Rome from the Fontana Paola on the Janiculum hill, with the King Victor Emmanuel II monument showing prominently. This is one of the best overviews of Rome looking eastward across the Tiber.*

RIGHT: *The Ponte Sant' Angelo, Rome, leading across the Tiber to the Castel Sant' Angelo, once the Emperor Hadrian's tomb. Three arches of the original bridge built by Hadrian's successor survive. In 1688 the bridge was extended and embellished with new parapets surmounted by ten angels designed by Bernini.*

Locorotondo and Martina Franca, we find the *trulli*, small rectangular or round houses with conical roofs built entirely from limestone blocks taken from the neighbourhood. The houses are whitewashed inside and out, the roofs go grey with weathering and the general effect in a countryside of olive and almond trees and vineyards is entrancing. In the Salentine peninsula (the heel of Italy), which begins just south of Alberobello, is the remarkably elegant city of Lecce, the paragon of southern Baroque architecture.

Throughout southern Italy and Sicily there were established from 1000 BC onwards, beginning with Cumae near Naples, a large number of Greek settlements reaching down to Reggio Calabria, then thrusting up northward along the Ionian coast and the Gulf of Taranto to Locri, Croton, Sybaris, Metapontum and Taranto, and westward across the Strait of Messina into Sicily. The whole area was known as Magna Graecia. One of the finest views in Italy, and indeed in the Mediterranean, is obtained from the Greek theatre in Taormina, Sicily. From a terrace 300 metres (1000 feet) above the sea, it embraces the Sicilian shore to Catania in front and the Calabrian coast on the left with the huge snow-capped mass of Mount Etna on the right. The nineteenth-century writer John Addington Symonds described it as the loveliest landscape on which his eyes had ever rested, 'a symphony of blues, gem-like lapis lazuli in the sea, aerial azure in the distant headlands, light irradiated sapphire in the sky and the impalpable vapour-mantled purple upon Etna'.

The Sicilian landscape, with its spaciousness and, in coastal areas at least, distant views of bare mountains and tranquil seas, is an ideal setting for

RIGHT: *The superb view out to sea from the grounds of the Villa Rufolo, a fascinating complex of Norman-Saracenic buildings with gardens and terraces, at Ravello on the coast south of Naples.*

the gravity of Greek temples. In some of the valleys of the centre, however, there are areas of green and gentle vegetation, such as the wooded country round the famous Roman villa of Piazza Armerina. There is also every sign of fertility in the Conca d'Oro, the beautiful plain round Palermo, and on the almond-covered slopes of Etna, which in blossom time seem to mirror the snows above.

Some of the finest of the Greek temples in the Mediterranean were built by Cretans, Rhodians and Megarians at Agrigento and Selinunte on the south coast of Sicily. The Temple of Concord at Agrigento is the best preserved of all Greek temples, with the exception of the Theseion in Athens. Another outstanding example, on the way north towards Palermo, is the Doric temple of Segesta, which stands alone on a terrace of land in front of a mountain and is also very well preserved and imposing in its solitary grandeur.

The road from Segesta to Palermo passes the Norman town of Monreale, which grew up around the remarkable cathedral erected by King William II (1172–6), and enters Palermo by the Porta Nuova leading to the Piazza Pretoria near the centre of the city. It is now a city struggling to rid itself of the incubus of the Mafia, but it has had an extraordinarily diverse and at times glorious history. It was occupied in turn by Romans, Byzantines, Saracens, Normans, German

ABOVE: *Alberobello, Apulia, has the greatest number of the trulli (stone houses with conical roofs) found only in this region of Italy.*

RIGHT: *The Piazza Roma in Martina Franca, Apulia, with its Baroque fountain and attractive garden, is overlooked by the Palazzo del Duca (1668) by Giovanni Andrea Carducci.*

BELOW: *The collegiate church of San Martino, with its elaborate Leccese Baroque entrance porch, and the Piazza Plebiscito, Martina Franca.*

emperors, Angevins, Aragonese, Spaniards, Neapolitans, French, English, North Italians and, during the last war, by the Americans. During the Norman occupation of Palermo it was the largest and wealthiest city, apart from Constantinople, under a Christian government anywhere. Some of the foreign occupiers, and the Normans especially, left behind them a noble artistic heritage.

It is worth noting that the inhabitants sited their buildings, whether in town or country, with a great gift for selecting the best positions and adapting to them with skill and sensitivity. A town on a river has one deportment; those by the sea or on a hill have another. The beauty of the Italian landscape has been enhanced by the hand of man.

LEFT: *The temple of Segesta in Sicily is a superb example of Doric architecture of the late fifth century BC. Its massive size and isolation (though nowadays close to some major roads) have made it a striking feature of the landscape.*

BELOW: *The view of Mount Etna from the Greek theatre at Taormina in Sicily.*

ARCHITECTURE

ABOVE: *Capital in the cloister (completed 1257) of the Cistercian abbey of Piona at the north-eastern end of Lake Como.*

LEFT: *Santa Maria della Consolazione, Todi, (Umbria), one of the finest examples of early Renaissance architecture, was begun in 1508 by Cola da Caprarola and completed (1516-24) by Ambrogio Marocci of Milan and Vito Lombardo.*

ARCHITECTURE

*T*he history of Italian architecture records a progression in which the influences and ideas from the world outside Italy were repeatedly applied, then adopted and transformed, and finally improved; in some instances they were then exported abroad as the pattern for adoption elsewhere. It will be best to ignore the artistic influences discernible in the peninsula during prehistoric times, which are still the subject of dispute, and to start with the period of Etruscan rule (616–509 BC), which extended from the Po Valley to the Gulf of Salerno.

The Etruscans were prodigious builders, but we have inherited a more lively idea of their art from the tombs they prepared for their dead than from the houses they built for the living. There are nevertheless sufficient remains of Etruscan temples, for example that of the Capitoline Jupiter (509 BC) in Rome, to afford us an idea of what these buildings were like, and to enlarge our

The Doric Temple of Neptune at Paestum near Salerno is one of the largest and best preserved of the Greek temples in Italy. It was built in the fifth century BC when Paestum was a thriving Greek colony called Poseidon.

architectural vocabulary by the use of an expression, the Tuscan order, referring to columns without bases, fluting or triglyphs. The rule of the Etruscan kings left its mark on Roman society in the religious, social and artistic spheres. Etruscan artists had been strongly influenced by Greek models and thus became a means by which the Romans formed their attachment for Greek art.

After the Romans had shaken off the Etruscan

yoke with the capture of Veii in 396 BC, the contact with the Greeks could be maintained through the settlements of Magna Graecia in southern Italy, a number of which had been founded about 750 BC. Other Greek colonies of importance were established in Sicily and along the shores of the Tyrrhenian Sea and beyond Calabria to the east. A few of the Greek settlements became thriving cities and cultural centres. In such places were built some of the most beautiful Greek temples in the Mediterranean.

The most impressive group of these on the mainland to have survived from the classical age of Greek architecture is in Paestum, the site of the Greek town of Poseidon, which was founded in the sixth century BC by emigrants from Sybaris. This place is about 65 kilometres (40 miles) down the coast from Salerno in what used to be a deserted plain but is now to some extent built over, with a large car park opposite the main temple. The largest of these temples is now called after Neptune, though believed to have been dedicated to Hera, the wife of Zeus. It is one of the best preserved with its thirty-six fine fluted

Among the finest of the impressive group of temples at Selinunte in Sicily is this Doric example in the eastern group (480-490 BC) with many of its pillars now reconstructed after an earthquake in 1958. The temple was probably dedicated to Hera.

columns, each five times the height of its diameter, with the gable half the height of a column. These were the measurements which yielded perfect proportion. A large temple nearby, erroneously called the Basilica though probably also dedicated to Hera, and a smaller very elegant one called the Temple of Ceres together with the Temple of Neptune, were all of the Doric order.

Other Greek temples are to be seen in Sicily. The temple of Segesta (fifth- to sixth-century BC) near Palermo stands alone in a bare and rocky landscape, very striking in its simplicity and solitude. The temples at Selinunte on the south coast are a group of five, among which the very large site of the Temple of Apollo (sixth century BC) is conspicuous because the only one of its columns to have remained standing is about 15 metres (50 feet) high, while others lie on the ground like stricken giants. Finally, at Agrigento, also on the south coast, the Valley of Temples runs down to the sea enclosing another remarkable group of three Doric temples, including the wonderfully preserved Temple of Concord (fifth century BC) and the ruins of the great Temple of Olympian Zeus, the largest Doric temple known, built from 480 BC onwards. The Greek influence on Roman architecture, transmitted through the Etruscans and through the Greeks of Magna Graecia, was compelling and many of the major buildings in Italy right through the Hellenistic period till the end of the Roman Republic were built by architects trained in the Greek style.

Nevertheless, in the latter part of the last century before our era, a new style in building was beginning to develop as a result of changes in Roman society. The wealth of the upper class, not merely of the landowners but of a number of successful professional men in the civilian and

The temple in the background, seen through the columns of the Temple of Neptune, is the oldest at Paestum (c.550 BC). It was misnamed the Basilica in the eighteenth century.

TOP: *The highly decorative mosaic of Neptune and Amphitrite at Herculaneum, a Greco-Roman seaside resort, which like Pompeii was completely engulfed by an eruption of Vesuvius in AD 79.*

ABOVE: *A shrine in the House of the Skeleton at Herculaneum.*

LEFT: *The Emperor Hadrian's Villa near Tivoli included this large waterway surrounded by columns and statues, a reminder of the Canopus canal near Alexandria in Egypt.*

fighting services and in commerce, had grown enormously from the booty acquired in conquering and administering the empire. With the increase of wealth came the taste for display and fine houses.

Within Rome itself, there were the imperial palaces with their fine gardens on the Palatine, and Maecenas, who was an extraordinarily rich man, had a palatial villa on another hill, the Esquiline. Tiberius' palace on the cliff-tops at Capri enjoyed from the beginning a scandalous reputation, after the lascivious life enjoyed there by the emperor was described by Suetonius. But of all the country retreats contrived by wealthy men, none was so grand and so beautifully adorned as Hadrian's Villa at Tivoli. There between AD 118 and 138, in that docile and not very interesting countryside where the plain joins the first slopes of the Tiburtine hills, the Spanish emperor, according to early classical historians, moulded the landscape over an area nearly the size of Hyde Park to resemble the most beautiful places he had seen during his travels: to the south he excavated the valley of the Canopus to remind him of the Egyptian Canopus Valley near Alexandria, to the north he set his reconstruction of the Greek Valley of Tempe and in between, in addition to a vast imperial palace, he built a version of the Stoa Poikile in Athens as well as other buildings suggesting a Greek inspiration. More recent research, however, has shown there is no actual resemblance, although the villa is certainly a vast complex of residential quarters, including barracks, nympheums, baths, theatres and libraries, each section being a self-contained unit, but every part integrated to some extent in the whole by the numerous pools and watercourses.

On the other hand, the wealth of Rome also attracted a large number of immigrants from the countryside and from abroad. During the reign of the Emperor Augustus (27 BC–AD 14) the population of Rome had reached upward of one

million inhabitants and the need for popular housing became urgent. The economy of the empire was dependent on a foundation of slavery, and the proletariat of Rome was composed of slaves (who in some rare cases were wealthy) and of impoverished citizens, who in many cases were very poor. To maintain the authority of government it was necessary to respond to the needs of the people.

The Roman rulers being very practical men responded to these needs with a variety of

The Largo Argentina in Rome is a town square with the ruins of four Roman temples at its centre, the earliest of which is thought to date from the third or fourth century BC.

buildings whose architecture was well devised to satisfy them. For the well-to-do they devised a type of home, the *domus*, which was an adaptation of Greek models; for the very poor the high-rising *insulae*, or blocks of flats; and for everybody's diversion the amphitheatres, theatres and circuses. For state ceremonial they built the curia and the

The mosaic in the apse of the sixth-century church of Sant' Apollinare in Classe near Ravenna is a symbolic representation of the Transfiguration of Christ on Mount Tabor. The colouring of each part of the composition is amazingly vivid but maintains a perfect harmony throughout. The style still shows a residue of classical naturalism which was to diminish when the outlook of the artists became purely Byzantine.

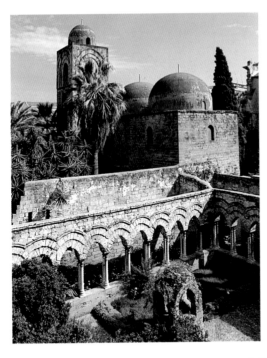

RIGHT : The capitals in
the twelfth-century cloister
of the Benedictine
monastery of Monreale near
Palermo in Sicily represent
themes from the Bible and
also agricultural and
hunting scenes, birds,
animals and plants. Some
are purely decorative.

ABOVE: Built during the
reign of King Roger II
(1130-54), San Giovanni
degli Eremiti in Palermo is
one of the best examples of
the Norman influence on
art in Sicily. Here
Byzantine domes, Norman
arches and Saracenic
ceilings seem to combine
without any clash of styles.

RIGHT: Intricacy vies
with simplicity as a means
to achieve perfection in the
cloister at Monreale, Sicily,
which contains 114 pairs
of slender columns of the
most varied design with
finely carved capitals. The
arches and some of the
geometric design in the
archivolts are Saracenic.

temples (the remains of four of the earliest examples of these, going back to the fourth or third century BC in the case of the oldest, are to be seen in the Largo Argentina in Rome). For the administration of law and the discussion of business they provided basilicas, and for the divinity of the emperor a panoply of monuments and more temples. Roman architecture, in all these forms, was to bequeath models to be used and re-adapted by many future generations.

The best-preserved examples of the Roman-style house are to be found in Pompeii and particularly in Herculaneum. The basic layout of the *domus* is a main room called the *atrium*, covered by a tiled roof sloping down towards the centre and with an opening wide enough to admit the necessary light for the *atrium* itself and the rooms giving on to it. This hole called the *compluvium* drained off its water into a basin, or *impluvium*, in the middle of the *atrium*. Beyond the *atrium* were the master bedroom (*tablinum*), the other bedrooms (*cubicula*), the reception rooms (*oeca*), the dining room (*triclinium*) and kitchen. There were no windows on the outside of the house.

Privacy was sacrosanct. Apart from the entrance, the front and often the sides of the house were let off for shops. The heating when required was by braziers with charcoal. Some houses of larger or wealthier families had two storeys and water could be carried up to the higher floor by leaden pipes. The houses were often richly decorated. In the house in Herculaneum named the house of Neptune and Amphitrite the bedroom gives on to an open *triclinium*, with a grotto nearby embellished with mosaics. A wall near this grotto is covered by a beautiful mosaic of the two naked deities standing side by side in a highly coloured frame of tendril decorations.

It was not in houses such as these that the less wealthy and the poor people of ancient Rome were accommodated. For such, when they were lucky enough to have a roof over their heads, it

The ceiling of St Mark's, Venice, showing the Cupola of Pentecost above the nave with the apostles preaching the gospel to the nations. The walls are entirely covered by an expanse of mosaic about an acre in area, which was put in place from the twelfth to the eighteenth centuries.

was the *insulae* which provided shelter. These were blocks of flats built mostly of bricks, some as high as six or seven floors; none of them, however, has survived in Rome, though some have been discovered in Ostia. They emerge for us, not very comfortably, in the pages of Roman historians and satirists. Without much light, without running water or drainage on the upper floors, sweltering hot in summer and icy cold in winter, they cannot have helped to alleviate the burden of straitened circumstances. Each floor of the *insula* was divided into apartments, access to which was gained from outside staircases. The plain front of the building was pierced by large windows. The ground floor was usually let off to shopkeepers. Some have seen in the *insula* a source of the urban architecture of Italy in the Middle Ages, with the use of unadorned brick façades for ordinary housing.

For the diversion of the people, the emperor developed to a high degree a variety of public spectacles, the chariot races in the circuses, the plays in the theatres, which were much larger than any operating in our day (the theatre of Marcellus could seat 14,000), and, most popular of all, the shows in the arena of the Colosseum.

This building rises in three bands of arcades, the arches supported by half-columns of the classical orders, Doric below, Ionic between and Corinthian on top, surmounted by a fourth band of slender Corinthian pilasters and small windows in a stone screen. The Colosseum could accommodate over 50,000 spectators, with seats for 45,000. Apart from its high aesthetic quality, it also embodied Roman efficiency in its design, providing convenient viewing and mobility for the vast audience which could be very rapidly

LEFT: *The Dominican church of Santa Maria Novella, Florence, has a patterned marble facing instead of the stone carving typical of Romanesque architecture in other parts of Tuscany. The lower part of this façade is fourteenth century, while the entablature, designed by Leon Battista Alberti, was built between 1456 and 1570.*

BELOW LEFT: *The pointed Saracenic arches of the Chiostro del Paradiso, Amalfi Cathedral, indicate an Arab inspiration, although this delightful retreat was commissioned by the Archbishop Augustariccio (1266-8) as a cemetery for deserving citizens.*

BELOW: *In spite of its comparatively recent foundation in 1240 by the Emperor Frederick II, L'Aquila, the capital of the mountainous province of Abbruzzo in central Italy, contains some remarkable monuments. The most original is the Romanesque church of Santa Maria di Collemaggio, shown here, which was completed in 1287.*

ABOVE: *San Michele in Lucca displays many of the characteristics of Tuscan or Pisan Romanesque style: blind arcading, extensive sculptural decoration and the stepped arcade on the gable front. The church was built in the eleventh and twelfth centuries but the mainly arcaded sections are of the fourteenth century.*

RIGHT: *One of the finest pulpits in Italy is in the cathedral of Ravello near Amalfi. It was commissioned by a local noble and made in 1272 by Nicola da Bartolomeo de Foggia, who was a master craftsman though little is known about him.*

evacuated after the show through no less than 160 *vomitoria*, or exits. The Emperor Titus arranged for the *munera*, or shows, for the inauguration of the Colosseum to last for a hundred days.

One other great example of Roman art must be mentioned because, like the Colosseum, it became an object of inspiration and of study for future generations of architects. This is the Pantheon in Rome. The Romans did not invent the arch or the vault, but they made such extensive and inventive use of both these devices

in the construction of buildings that they could rightfully claim to have made revolutionary advances in architecture. The Pantheon, as rebuilt by the Emperor Hadrian between AD 124 and 128, is the supreme example in Roman imperial architecture of the construction of a great dome. Here a characteristic of Roman skill, in combining good engineering with an appetite for grandiosity, is used to the maximum effect. The dome has served as an inspiration for later architects like Palladio and Bernini, and its size was not surpassed until the engineer-architect Pier Luigi Nervi built the Sports Palace for the Roman Olympic Games in 1960 with reinforced concrete.

There is still another type of Roman building which must be mentioned here because it has occupied such a conspicuous place in the history of subsequent architecture in Italy. This was the basilica, whose origin is obscure. The basilica was a large, covered, rectangular hall containing an inner hall surrounded by columns. Basilicas were used as meeting places for the crowds gathered in the forum to shelter from the glare of summer sunshine, from sudden drenching rain, or the icy Tramontana wind as it blew down from the mountains in winter. They were places for meeting friends and gossiping, or for transacting legal and commercial business. In later times they were often used to house the law courts.

The chief novel traits of Roman architecture may be summarised as follows: there was a general emphasis on the practical uses of public buildings like markets or baths in construction programmes (though the continuing taste for triumphal arches constituted a notable exception to this tendency); there was also a greater awareness of the decorative possibilities of the interiors of buildings, which included the importance of a striking façade to focus attention on the comforts within. Then new techniques of building – the development of vaults and domes, and the invention of new mixtures of concrete –

enabled the emperors to construct buildings of hitherto unimaginable size and grandeur.

During the reign of Constantine, after the repeal of the laws against Christianity (AD 313), a number of Christian churches were founded. Many of these were basilicas, though not all. One of the most striking of the latter is Santa Costanza in Rome, built as an imperial family tomb for a saint not quite satisfactorily identified as Costanza or Constantina. It is the first Christian monument to have been built as such in Italy which has

The beautiful abbey of Vezzolano was completed in 1169 in the Lombard Romanesque fashion, except for the blind arcading on the front of the church reminiscent of the churches of Pisa and Lucca.

survived structurally undamaged. It is a round building, not a basilica, with a dome resting on a succession of arches supported on columns, a novelty for that time. In the vault of the ambulatory are some of the finest mosaics of the outstanding Roman mosaic artists of the period.

The example of church building set by Constantine was followed up by the popes who gained in power and wealth through the withdrawal of the emperor from Rome and the large donations of land made by him and by his successors to the Holy See. During this time the classical spirit remained strong.

A notable example of the new churches is Santa Maria Maggiore, built by Pope Sixtus III (AD 432–40). One of the seven major Christian basilicas in Rome, it is the oldest and the most

splendid. The entablature above the arches is formed by a long mosaic band illustrating scenes from the Old Testament with remarkable vivacity. These, together with the mosaics covering the monumental archway into the sanctuary, and those surrounding the high altar recounting Christ's early life, represent the best Roman mosaic work of the fifth century. Some may be examples of the Church's use of art for the spread of its doctrine, in this case the scenes glorifying the Virgin Mary to counter the Nestorian view of

The Cistercian monastery at Follina in the Veneto was founded in the twelfth century but the cloister was not completed until 1268. It is in Romanesque style with arches supported on graceful twinned columns beneath a wide banded architrave.

there being two separate persons in Christ and their denial that the Virgin Mary was the mother of God as well as of Christ.

The fifth century, in which the harmonious beauty of Santa Maria Maggiore was created, also

witnessed the invasion and sacking of Rome by the barbarians. Italy suffered severe hardship from this and other invasions but also derived considerable benefit from the Byzantine rule which followed them and which left a clear mark in widely different areas of the peninsula. Although Byzantine art emerged most directly from Roman and Greek antecedents, it also contained elements of Eastern, mostly Syrian, influence. The essence of Byzantine art at its best was a fusion of elements from East and West.

There was, however, one influence which made the expression of Byzantine art markedly different from that of its predecessors and that was the Christian religion which, in the age of Justinian, was in many ways the intellectual bedrock of the Eastern empire. It was said that in the bazaar at Constantinople nobody would buy even a loaf of bread without engaging in an argument about a problem such as the nature of the Holy Trinity.

In Italy Byzantine architecture was represented very early on in the church of Sant' Apollinare in Classe near Ravenna, built from 531 to 536, slightly before the Emperor Justinian's capable general, Narses, had finally subdued the last resistance of the Goths in the peninsula. This church was a large basilica dedicated to Saint Apollinaris, the first Bishop of Ravenna. As you enter the wide nave of the church, you are immediately dazzled by the green and gold gleam of the mosaic in the apse where a bishop, his hands extended in prayer, stands beneath a deep blue mosaic circle enclosing a large cross. This is a symbol, truly Byzantine, of the Transfiguration of Christ on Mount Tabor and is the chief of a number of glorious mosaics by Byzantine artists around the church, all of which display the same exquisite sense of symmetry and colour.

At the other end of Italy, in Sicily at Palermo and the nearby small town of Monreale, the Byzantine influence was also paramount and, even many hundreds of years later, produced more dazzling displays of mosaic in churches built in what is called the Siculo-Norman architectural style. The Normans in Sicily were surprisingly tolerant rulers. They encouraged artistic inspiration from any quarter. In their piety they erected churches which were an amalgam of Saracenic arches and stalactitic roofs, of Romanesque naves, and of interior walls and vaults glowing with the gold and brilliant colouring of Byzantine mosaics. The church of San Giovanni degli Eremiti in Palermo, with a

The church of Pieve di Santa Maria in Arezzo, Tuscany, is one of the finest examples of Romanesque architecture in Italy with its beamed ceiling, high nave flanked by aisles, and clustered pillars.

cluster of red domes and a small courtyard enclosing a garden, was built in 1132 almost certainly by Arab craftsmen working under Norman architects for King Roger II of Sicily, whose court was the most distinguished centre of artistic patronage in Europe, while his capital was one of the wealthiest cities of the Continent.

For overwhelming splendour, however, we must look to the cathedral and monastery of Monreale, a small town not far south of Palermo, with its outstandingly beautiful cloister. Here,

once again, the three artistic traditions supplied by Arab, Byzantine and Italian artists were superbly harnessed by their Norman masters. The cathedral of Monreale was built by King William II from 1172 to 1176.

About a hundred years earlier (1063–79) in Venice the church of St Mark was being built to the design of a Greek architect. Byzantine influence in Venice remained very strong until the sack of Constantinople by the Crusaders in 1204 (due mainly to Venetian instigation), so the first

period of decoration was largely Byzantine. The construction saw an important innovation: the brick vaulting instead of wooden roofing. This made possible the covering of the whole interior with an unbroken adornment of mosaic. In some chapels there are signs of a transition to Gothic sculpture and in the baptistery to Gothic mosaic design. With the sacristy door modelled by Sansovino, we are confronted with the fully fledged Renaissance. St Mark's displays many styles but it is the Byzantine which predominates.

On the whole the influence of Byzantine art in

LEFT: *Sant' Eufemia in Spoleto, Umbria, was built in the first half of the twelfth century and is one of the best examples of Lombard Romanesque style in the region.*

BELOW: *Among the interesting features inside Sant' Eufemia, Spoleto, are the assortment of pillars and columns scavenged from ancient sites, the matroneum (women's gallery) and the thirteenth-century high altar with Comatesque mosaic work.*

Italy was exercised much more obviously in decoration, especially through mosaics, than in architecture. And while its repercussions were still active in southern Italy and in Venice, another far more prolific style was maturing in other parts of Italy, the Romanesque.

After the collapse of the Roman Empire of Charlemagne, Italy fell once more into one of her endemic periods of decadence. Again, however, the Italians showed their insuperable capacity for survival, stimulated and assisted by the one institution which was able to provide a moderate degree of cohesion, a certain measure of continuity and a sense of purpose – the Church. Towards the end of the millennium men turned their minds to the contemplation of spiritual things, and many new churches were built. It was then that the Italian Romanesque style was born.

Italian Romanesque architecture first appeared in Lombardy, Milan, Parma, Modena amongst other places. Distinctive features were shallow pilasters dividing up the outside curve of an apse, or other outside wall spaces, surmounted by dwarf pensile arcading below the roof, with a protruding pedimented porch and a bell tower nearby.

Among the most beautiful buildings in Italy are the church buildings in Pisa and Lucca, which make far more elaborate use of exterior decoration than was common in the churches of Lombardy. These, in the style called Tuscan Romanesque, include the most famous group of the cathedral and Camposanto of Pisa as well as the church of San Michele in Lucca. The latter's thirteenth-century arcaded façade is particularly impressive. A very different kind of Romanesque church is San Miniato al Monte (*c.*1090) in Florence. Here the beauty of the façade relies more on the pattern of inlaid coloured marble decoration than on architectural features like columns and arcades.

An interesting Romanesque church in Rome is Santa Maria in Cosmedin in the Forum Boarium,

ABOVE: *The pulpit by Giovanni Pisano in the church of Sant' Andrea in Pistoia, Tuscany, was completed in 1301. Six red marble columns standing on lions and human figures support the Gothic arches on which the pulpit rests, as well as dramatic figures of the prophets, and the outside parapet contains five sculptured panels with scenes depicting the life of Christ.*

RIGHT: *The Certosa di Pavia, Lombardy, seen from the small cloister. This part of the Certosa dates from the latter half of the fifteenth century and is in the Lombard style.*

or 'cattle market', of Ancient Rome. It was transformed into a church of the Romanesque style in the twelfth century when the architraves in the aisle arcades were replaced by round arches and a remarkably tall campanile was added. Some fine examples of Romanesque architecture can be seen in L'Aquila in the Abruzzi and at Ravello by the coastal stretch between Amalfi and Salerno.

compared to other western European countries, relatively few Italian Gothic buildings were of outstanding importance. In Rome and southern Italy resistance to the new style was instinctive. In northern and central Italy the spread of the style coincided with the period which followed the establishment of communal government in many cities, from about 1080 to 1150. Once their independence was assured they vied to create municipal buildings of a suitably massive appearance in the new style. This happened in the larger cities like Florence and Siena and also in small towns like Ascoli Piceno in the Marches.

Ecclesiastical buildings in the Gothic style are rarer, but some are certainly most notable like the cathedrals in Florence, Siena and Orvieto and the Cistercian abbey of Fossanova, south of Rome. The most ornate of all is the late Gothic cathedral of Milan. This is a remarkable building and among Italian churches second only in size to St Peter's in Rome. The cathedral was founded around 1386 and consecrated in 1577. Fifty architects contributed to its construction, among them French and Germans. Externally the stonework tracery of screens, arches, massed pillars, pinnacles, spires and finials; the flying buttresses with raked lines capped by sharp merlons and crockets; the vast Gothic windows below and small trefoil ones above; and the soaring steeple rising out of a huge, highly ornamented tower-lantern over the crossing make a somewhat overpowering impression. For many people, however, the cathedral of Milan is most striking on the inside where a clearer definition of its features, due to a less frenetic display of ornament, and the grandeur of its proportions, viewed in a subdued light, are arresting.

Where it occurred, the transition from Gothic to Renaissance architecture was certainly more abrupt a change than the move away from Romanesque. The Renaissance – a term of

There is one other area in Italy where Romanesque architecture flourished. This remarkably was in the region of Apulia. The impulse here was given by the bishops and abbots of the main cities and abbeys of the region. This happened in a time of expanding economy, with Bari, Otranto and Taranto becoming centres of east–west trade. Bari was also a main embarkation port for pilgrimages to the Holy Land. Thus spiritual motivation and economic strength were

harnessed in Apulia to sustain a major building programme which was almost entirely ecclesiastical and produced some of the finest Romanesque art in Italy. Examples are the cathedrals of Bari, Trani and Troia. Sicily under Norman rule also produced wonderful Romanesque cathedrals like those of Monreale, Palermo and Cefalù.

One cannot assert that the Gothic style superseded the Romanesque in Italy because,

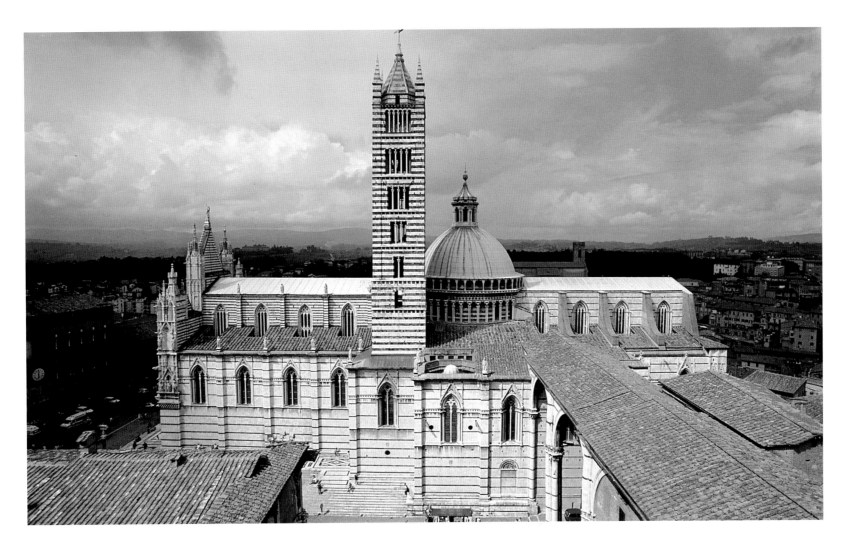

Considered by many to be the finest of the Italian Gothic cathedrals, Siena Cathedral was begun in 1196 and completed in the second half of the fourteenth century. The façade was built by Giovanni Pisano and the Sienese Giovanni di Lecco.

general application to indicate changes in art and culture – began in Florence early in the fifteenth century and spread gradually to Rome and Venice and then to the whole of Europe.

With the waning of the Middle Ages there occurred a deep revival of interest in the study of the classics, especially at the court of Cosimo de' Medici, who founded an academy in Florence for the study of Plato. After the fall of Constantinople to the Turks in 1453 a number of Greek scholars sought refuge in Italy and enhanced Italian scholars' knowledge of Greek texts. Meanwhile the study of the Roman classics received fresh impetus from the development of printing and the discovery of new texts. Among the latter the handbook on architecture by the Roman M. Vitruvius Pallio of the last century BC acquired great authority among Italian architects; in it Vitruvius formulated the axiom that beauty in architecture was achieved by creating a harmony in the proportions of each part of a building, based on a fixed module for the parts and for the whole.

One of the great practitioners of this axiom was the brilliant scholar and humanist, Leon Battista Alberti (1404–1472). He wrote a treatise, *De Re Aedificatoria*, which was immensely influential as a handbook of theory and practice for architects up till the eighteenth century. Even before the publication of *De Re Aedificatoria*, one of the greatest architectural geniuses of any age, Filippo Brunelleschi, was producing his reinterpretation of Roman architecture *all'antica* with his exquisitely proportioned and classically perfect Ospedale degli Innocenti (an orphanage) in Florence (1419–1424), and expanding his knowledge of medieval building design by the daring structural

techniques which he employed. These can be seen in his completion of the soaring dome of the cathedral of Santa Maria del Fiore, Florence, without the use of centring (internal scaffolding to prop up the inside of the interior dome while the mortar hardened). With this prominent dome he created an outstanding focal point in the visual unity of Florence among the tall buildings of the city centre and the surrounding hills and valley.

Though the Ospedale degli Innocenti shows

Madonna di San Biagio (1518-45) outside Montepulciano, Tuscany, is the masterpiece of Antonio da Sangallo the Elder. A simple but elegant Renaissance structure of travertine stone, it is built in the shape of a Greek cross, with a fine cupola and classical façade.

traces of derivation from Tuscan Romanesque models, its main feature, the loggia front, displays such strong links with classical Roman architecture as to present a perfectly distinct style

and it is generally recognised as a prototype of Renaissance architecture. Curiously enough, though, this external loggia was used as a standard feature of the interior courtyards of the hundreds of Renaissance palaces which it inspired and not as a model for their façades.

If Brunelleschi's role may be described as transitional between Gothic/Romanesque and Renaissance architecture, and Alberti's as theoretically fundamental, the real establishment

RIGHT: *The Ospedale del Ceppo, Pistoia, was founded in 1227 as an old people's home, and the loggia which is now the façade was built in about 1480. It was decorated by Giovanni della Robbia and others with medallions and terracotta panels, and completed in the 1580s.*

RIGHT: *The façade of Sant' Agostino, Montepulciano, was designed by the Florentine Michelozzo di Bartolomeo in 1472. He had a tendency to mingle classical and Gothic forms in his work.*

LEFT: *The sanctuary of the Madonna dei Miracoli at Lonigo in the Veneto (1488) has a Lombardic façade with heavily mullioned windows, and the upper part is decorated with volute-like shells.*

of the Renaissance style in Florence was effected by later architects who built the palaces of the rising class of merchant bankers, with the Medici in the lead. The general plan of these palaces is beautifully illustrated by Michelozzo Michelozzi's Palazzo Medici (1444–59). It was a three-storeyed building with a wide cornice on top and a large square central courtyard with, on the ground floor, an open arcade on each side like sections of Brunelleschi's hospital that are set at right angles to each other.

The outside walls of palazzi at this stage were strongly rusticated as is seen in Benedetto da Maiano's Palazzo Strozzi (1489–1536). Many Florentine Renaissance palaces followed the plan of the Palazzo Medici. Some were renewed in the seventeenth and eighteenth centuries or given a new façade like that of Palazzo Peruzzi by Gherardo Silvani in the seventeenth century.

It was from the beginning of the sixteenth century that the Early Renaissance of Florence developed into the High Renaissance of Rome in which, however, none of the leading architects was Roman. Donato Bramante, who built the exquisite small temple (1502) in the courtyard of San Pietro in Montorio, was an Umbrian; Raphael, who was the architect of the Palazzo Vidoni (1515), was from Urbino; Antonio da Sangallo the Younger and Michelangelo, who between them completed most of the Palazzo Farnese (1514–89), the finest High Renaissance palazzo in Rome, were Florentine as was Baldassare Peruzzi, though born in exile and raised in Siena.

It was Peruzzi who designed the Palazzo Massimo alle Colonne (1481–1536), generally considered one of the most important buildings in the new style later called Mannerism. This abandoned the rigid perfection of Early Renaissance

ABOVE: *The Villa Rotonda (1566-70) near Vicenza, perhaps the most famous of the villas by Palladio, was completed with a* flattened dome by Vincenzo Scamozzi in 1580.

ABOVE AND RIGHT: *The façade and internal arcade of the Loggia di Davide, which is the eastern wing of the Palazzo del Tè, Mantua. This vast palazzo was built (c.1530) for Frederick II Gonzaga, Duke of Mantua, by the Roman painter and architect Giulio Romano. It is perhaps the most illustrious building in the Mannerist style, where the emphasis is on ornament as well as variety and irregularity.*

*The Teatro Olimpico at
Sabbioneta, a Gonzaga
stronghold in Lombardy,
was built in 1590 for
Vespasiano Gonzaga by
Vincenzo Scamozzi. The
theatre, which was
influenced by Palladio's
Teatro Olimpico in
Vicenza, contains many
interesting and attractive
elements inspired by the
theatres of classical
antiquity. During the
Renaissance, architects were
often called on by their
patrons to provide for the
entertainment of the courts
by building theatres and
theatrical sets and scenery
for the performance of
plays, and later, opera.*

classicism by introducing surprises into the orderly progress of a classical design. The Palazzo Massimo with its curved façade to accommodate a bend in the road and its deeply inset, colonnaded entrance defies the canons of Renaissance full frontal dignity, but it is enchanting.

The new style achieved its apotheosis in Giulio Romano's Palazzo del Tè (1525–35) built in Mantua for Federico Gonzaga II, one of the great patrons of the arts in the sixteenth century. Giulio Pippi, known as Giulio Romano, was one of the very few indigenous Roman artists of really high merit. He was one of Raphael's brightest assistants in the painting of the Vatican Stanze and Loggias. The Mannerist mood gained his adherence later and is clearly seen in different sections of the Palazzo del Tè like the slumped triglyphs in the frieze and the broken pediments over the windows of the north side of the Court of Honour, or the agitated pictorial illusionism of the Sala dei Giganti. It was admired by contemporaries like Vasari in 1541 and other well-known architects and painters of the Renaissance followed this trend. Much later it was energetically denounced as the complete annihilation of form by the Swiss art historian Heinrich Wölfflin in his book *Renaissance und Barock* (1888).

In the 1560s a new artistic genius in the classical mould revealed himself with a vision combining simplicity and grandeur, Andrea Palladio of Padua. He was, among Italian architects, the one who had more influence abroad than any other. In his great Venetian churches of San Giorgio and the Redentore Palladio revived the classical purity of Renaissance building without sacrificing effects, like his use of Istrian white stone and whitewashed stucco. And in his villas in the Veneto he set an example of grandiose perfection which has not been equalled again in Italy.

Towards the end of the sixteenth century interest in Mannerism faded rapidly. There was, however, a lingering taste for the freedom which it had procured from a rigid acceptance of the Vitruvian rules. What replaced it was the Baroque style, which combined a recognition of the fundamental importance of classical conceptions in architecture with a considerable freedom in applying them. This freedom was accompanied by the intention to produce excitement and emotion in the beholder, which was not a principal aim of the Renaissance architect.

The new style, like the Gothic, Renaissance and Mannerist styles, acquired its name from later writings – in this case by Jacob Burckhardt and Wölfflin in the nineteenth century. It was in use throughout the seventeenth century and evolved into the Rococo style of the next century. From Rome it spread throughout Italy and Europe with astonishing speed, perhaps because it involved the emotion of the spectators and allowed great freedom to the creators of works of art, of whom Gianlorenzo Bernini was one of the most important. His masterpieces as a sculptor are famous and, as the architect of the Scala Regia in the Vatican and the Colonnade of St Peter's, his work is seen by thousands of new admirers every day. But it is in the diminutive church of Sant' Andrea al Quirinale, shaped like a bantam's egg, opposite the Quirinal Palace in Rome, that his singular talent is most attractively displayed and where the Baroque element of his artistry is most clearly demonstrated. Here he would, in his old age, console himself about his achievement for he tended to be critical of his own works and from this one he derived the greatest satisfaction.

The Villa Rosa, Tramonte, in the Veneto was built in the early eighteenth century and is famed for the beauty of its wrought-iron gates.

ABOVE: *The Sala degli Specchi in the Palazzo Carrega Cataldi, one of a number of sumptuous palaces erected by wealthy merchants in the Via Garibaldi, Genoa, about the middle of the sixteenth century. The architect for much of the Baroque decoration is thought to have been G. B. Castello, but this extraordinary room was the work of Lorenzo de Ferrari.*

LEFT: Trompe l'oeil *architectural effects in the Sala dell' Inverno of the Palazzo Rosso, Genoa, which was built (1671–7) for the Brignole family by, it is claimed, the architect Antonio Corradi of Como. This salon, one of a suite in the palazzo depicting the seasons, has a ceiling fresco (1687–9) by Domenico Piola representing the Allegory of Winter.*

Bernini's great rival in Rome was Francesco Borromini, a Lombard from Lake Lugano, who arrived in Rome in 1614 at the age of fifteen and worked as a stonemason at St Peter's and the Palazzo Barberini until commissioned by the Theatine congregation to build their church of San Carlo alle Quattro Fontane (completed in 1667). Only a stone's throw away from Bernini's Sant' Andrea (completed in 1670), this was an awkward site on which Borromini moulded his small church in a series of highly intricate undulations to secure an enthralling Baroque effect. His other masterpiece in Rome was the even more complicated church of Sant' Ivo della Sapienza (1642–60), which appears to herald the advent of the Rococo style.

Two more outstanding architects of the Baroque style must be mentioned. The first was Pietro da Cortona, a painter and architect from Tuscany. One of the most attractive church exteriors in Rome is that of Santa Maria della Pace which he built in 1656–7, where the convex curve of the façade is counteracted by the concave curvature of the surrounding building. The second is Baldassare Longhena, who designed the church of Santa Maria della Salute (1631–81) in Venice, unquestionably one of the most glorious buildings in the Baroque style, with its ingenious transformation of the buttresses supporting the dome into a series of giant scrolls with the twelve apostles standing on top of them.

A late and altogether astonishing manifestation of Baroque occurred from the end of the sixteenth to the end of the eighteenth centuries in the southernmost region of Apulia. Its centre was the provincial capital of Lecce, an attractive and civilised city of great cultural distinction, with its own university, which earned for itself the appellation of the Florence of the South. The Roman Baroque style was introduced into the deep south by the religious orders of the Jesuits and the Theatines, who found in Lecce two

favourable factors for the promotion of their architectural aspirations – a group of brilliant architects and a honey-coloured stone, the *pietra leccese*. This was abundant in the quarries round about and was very easy to carve but became hard with weathering. The most renowned of the local architects were Gabriele Riccardi, active from 1524–86; Giuseppe Zimbalo, who rebuilt the cathedral (1659–70) and designed the church of Santa Croce (1646); and Achille Carducci who built the church of San Matteo (1667–1700) – all fine examples of the Leccese Baroque.

With the gradual diminution of great architects in Italy during the eighteenth century, a new style was for a short time imported from France to provide a fresh outlook on the architectural scene. This was the Rococo style which flourished in France in the reign of King Louis XV. It did not become widespread in Italy or achieve the same perfection as in France or Germany except in the French-orientated court of Victor Amadeus II of Savoy. One masterpiece by a great eclectic architect, the Sicilian Filippo Juvarra who worked for many years at the court in Turin, has survived in the palatial hunting lodge at Stupinigi. Here, in a number of rooms in different suites, particularly in the great central ballroom, the Rococo inventiveness of the architect and his assistant painters, plasterers and cabinet-makers vies with the showpieces of this style in France and in Germany. At the other end of the country in Sicily there also appeared some surprising eruptions of Rococo architecture.

The revival of interest in the art of classical antiquity, fuelled by the excavations of the Roman ruins in Pompeii and Herculaneum since 1748, and the passion of the great German art historian Winckelmann (1717–68), led to the foundation of the Neoclassical movement in Rome. It soon spread throughout Italy and was much in vogue for public buildings and monuments. Some of the Italian opera houses, notably the Scala in Milan by Giuseppe Piermarini (1776–8) and Carlo Barabino's fine Teatro Carlo Felice in Genoa (1826-8), are among the better examples; some of the huge public monuments, like that to King Victor Emmanuel II in Rome (1885–1911) by Giuseppe Sacconi, are among the worst. An eclectic Neoclassicism mingling with Baroque elements has remained popular. One builder, in the tradition of the great Roman engineer-architects, has achieved worldwide renown in this century: Pier Luigi Nervi.

Apart from the creation within Italy of beautiful buildings, Italian architects and decorators were often employed abroad, notably in France, Spain, Germany and Russia. The Palladian style was copied with much success in England and in America – from Lord Burlington's Chiswick House to Jefferson's Monticello in Charlottesville. It may, therefore, be claimed that no other country has made such a contribution to the development of architecture as Italy.

San Paolo fuori le Mura outside Rome is a nineteenth-century Neoclassical rebuilding of a basilica which was founded by Constantine in the fourth century, enlarged by subsequent emperors and destroyed by fire in 1823.

INTERIORS

ABOVE: *The dining room of a trullo in Alberobello, Apulia.*

LEFT: *The main salon in the Villa Cicogna Mozzoni, Lombardy.*

PALAZZO PERUZZI
Florence

The Palazzo Peruzzi and the attached medieval houses which belonged to the family are situated in the Piazza dei Peruzzi and the Via Borgo dei Greci between the Piazza della Signoria and the Piazza Santa Croce in Florence. In 1899 the palazzo was sold to the Grazzi family who are the present owners. The present palazzo is of the seventeenth century with a façade designed by Gherardo Silvani, the architect of the church of San Filippo Neri (1633) and of other notable buildings in Florence.

The Peruzzi were a prominent family of Florentine merchant bankers. As early as the middle of the twelfth century there is a reference in the records to a certain Ubaldino Peruzzi. By the fourteenth century the Peruzzi had become one of the main banking families in Europe. They were members of the élite club of mercantile families which controlled the Arte della Lana, or Wool Guild. However, the Peruzzi made the mistake of advancing 600,000 florins to King

Edward III of England to launch out on the Hundred Years' War against France. The king defaulted on this loan and on another even bigger advance by the Bardi bankers. In 1343 the Peruzzi failed and the Bardi a year later. The financial result on depositors was disastrous and one of the causes of Florence's gradual decline as a leader in the money market.

A further setback to the family occurred in the following century, when Ridolfo Peruzzi was sent into exile with his family for backing the Albizzi family against the Medici. A prominent member of the family was the architect and painter Baldassare Peruzzi, who was born in exile in Siena but worked mostly in Rome (1527–30) where he built the delightful Palazzo Massimo alle Colonne.

In 1783, following a marriage of Bindo Simone Peruzzi with Anna Maria de' Medici, the Peruzzi added the Medici name to their own. A descendant of this union was another Ubaldino Peruzzi, who during the nineteenth century was for a long time one of the Florentine deputies in the Italian parliament and twice a minister. He was Mayor of Florence in the 1860s when the city was capital of the Kingdom of Italy. During this period, when the interior decoration must have looked much as it is today, the palazzo was admirably suited to the grand style of entertainment which the mayor, Ubaldino, and his charming wife, Donna Emilia Peruzzi, lavished upon the cultural élite of Florence. Such

The entrance hall, with a white porcelain horse of German origin and an equestrian picture by English artist Thomas Franklin.

Detail of a sofa in the Salotto Rosso.

distinguished guests as the Lombard aristocrat and Minister for Foreign Affairs Visconti Venosta, and the author Edmondo De Amicis, would meet their hosts in the brightly decorated Salotto Rosso, equipped with nineteenth-century Florentine furniture in Empire style upholstered in red Florentine damask.

The dining room known as La Galleria is decorated by Attanasio Bimbaccio (c.1690) with scenes from family history depicted on the walls and the Apotheosis of Florence and Tuscany on the ceiling. The entrance hall is striking. Its fine chimneypiece is of the nineteenth century with an English sporting picture by Thomas Franklin on the mantelpiece and a large white porcelain horse from Germany in front of it. In the bedroom an unusual feature is a marble rotonda inlay on the floor with the owner's initials.

The Salotto Rosso, the main drawing room, with Empire-style furniture covered with red silk damask made in Florence.

ABOVE: *The small dining room, with fresco decoration by Attanasio Bimbaccio of Florence (c.1690).*

LEFT: *The Salotto Grigio, with walls and ceiling also frescoed by Bimbaccio.*

ABOVE: *The striking four-poster bed in the main bedroom is in the late eighteenth-century Empire style. The owner's initials are set in the floor.*

LEFT: *The spacious bathroom is not lacking in decoration, with glass jars and urns in a showcase and a painting on the wall.*

PALAZZO PANDOLFI-ELMI
Umbria

The region of Umbria with its gentle landscape is one of the most relaxing and attractive in Italy, although this peaceful atmosphere is sometimes shattered by the political faction fighting which erupts during elections in parts of the area. It is one of the most medieval places in Italy with a number of very beautiful small towns set among its hills. These towns, even though they harbour a strong industrial element, retain a large part of their medieval appearance. In origin, however, they are usually found to be Roman and to have had a role in guarding a route used by caravan traders. Some of these towns were also affected by the impulses of the Renaissance, and often the architecture of that period is interwoven into the city's fabric together with such styles as Roman, Romanesque, Gothic and other more modern styles.

The early sixteenth-century palazzo portrayed in the accompanying photographs was raised over the ruins of a medieval house. It is an example of the kind of mansion which members of the local nobility in an Umbrian town would build during

ABOVE: *Part of the ceiling of the Salone Rosso, with landscapes in the central medallions.*

LEFT: *The courtyard of this sixteenth-century palazzo is based on Florentine models of the previous century.*

RIGHT: *The Salone Rosso derives its name from its red floral wallpaper imported from Paris (c.1840). The floor is of highly polished brickwork set in squares. The vaulted ceiling and the walls were probably frescoed by Filippo Latari (active 1780-1820).*

LEFT: *A theatre was a fairly common feature of Italian palaces where amateur theatricals were a popular pastime.*

RIGHT: *La Alcova, which usually meant the alcove in a bedroom where the bed was concealed behind a curtain, but in some palaces it was a room reserved for love trysts.*

LEFT: *The Salone Verde, another drawing room but with green wallpaper from Paris. The frescoes are thought to be by Latari, an Umbrian painter and decorator who did much of his work in Rome.*

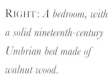

RIGHT: *A bedroom, with a solid nineteenth-century Umbrian bed made of walnut wood.*

the Renaissance, with later furnishing and decoration added by descendants. The interior courtyard is of the type established in Florence in the middle of the fifteenth century with the difference of leaving open the arcade on the first floor as a flower-laden terrace instead of enclosing it with windows.

As is usual with Renaissance palaces there is a variety of salons *en suite* some using a single dominating colour as their theme with often, as here, a Salone Rosso and a Salone Verde (Red and Green Drawing Rooms). The elegant Salone Rosso is adorned with landscapes and grotesques in the frescoes on the vaulted ceiling. The ceiling decoration is attributed to a well-known Umbrian painter Filippo Latari, active from 1780 to 1820, who was employed at times in the decoration of some of the Roman palaces. The furniture is bright red and of a comfortable-looking modernity. A very graceful doorway framed in

stucco moulding encloses floral decoration in the pediment. The Salone Verde contains a vaulted ceiling with vine and tasselled cordon decoration, also by Latari, while the walls are covered with a striking green, Parisian wallpaper with laurel wreath garlands round medallions and lozenges portraying landscapes and hunting scenes.

One feature of the palace, which is to be found in a number of large houses, is the Family Theatre. The need to express oneself dramatically

is deep-seated in the Italian people. Even everyday conversations in the streets are a theatrical performance, especially in the south. For each expression there is a nuance of gesture which gives a more precise or emphatic meaning. Sometimes no words are necessary to convey the thought. In the history of theatre the Italians hold a place of primary importance. It was Cardinal Rospigliosi, later Pope Clement IX, who produced the first comic opera script. In the houses of aristocracy as well as on the street the theatre is a part of life.

Another large room which bears the mysterious name of the Alcove (La Alcova) is a feature of a number of palaces, a place specially reserved as a trysting parlour for lovers. It has now been turned into a music room. Here there are rafters in the ceiling, while the light-coloured walls have an ingenious pattern of drapery and green garlands.

There are few pictures but the small Venetian mirrors in gold frames act as focal points on the walls. The furniture is of different styles and colours but creates a harmonious whole.

In the bedroom the large, nineteenth-century four-poster bed with hanging drapery over the headboard is made of walnut wood. This provincial palace displays considerable decorative and architectural distinction.

PALAZZO DEI CONTI DI LECCE
Apulia

The city of Lecce is the capital of a province of the same name in the Salentine peninsula at the south-eastern extremity of Italy. It is a town with a very ancient history which was occupied and rebuilt by the Romans in the third century BC. As usual, they built an amphitheatre, a theatre and a basilica. At its centre was a fort, the Castro. The garden of the Palazzo dei Conti di Lecce abuts on the Roman theatre. The palace is thought to have been built on the ruins of the fort, which would probably have been close to the chief monuments of the city. After the Gothic Wars of the sixth century, Lecce remained under Byzantine jurisdiction almost continuously for five centuries.

When the Normans conquered Apulia there was a great change. In 1056 Robert Guiscard was recognised by Pope Nicholas II as Duke of Apulia and Calabria. The territory in the province was divided among cities owing direct allegiance to the duke and others swearing fealty to a count. Lecce belonged to the latter category. During the period of Norman rule the province of Lecce gradually recovered from the scars of war. Lecce in particular became prosperous as a commercial centre.

The Norman counts of Lecce were succeeded by Swabian counts when German emperors ruled southern Italy. After the defeat of Conradin of Swabia by Charles of Anjou at Tagliacozzo in 1268, the Angevins obtained possession of Lecce and installed the Brienne family as its wardens. They ruled it until 1356, to be succeeded by the d'Enghien family. Later, in 1463, the County of Lecce was fully integrated into the Kingdom of Naples, which had meanwhile been taken over by Alfonso I of Aragon. Thereafter, in 1500, by the Treaty of Granada between France and Spain,

RIGHT: *The garden seen from the roof terrace.*

FAR RIGHT: *The courtyard, whose eighteenth-century Baroque façade is attributed to Emanuele Manieri, a son of the famous Leccese Baroque architect Mauro Manieri.*

Apulia was handed over to the latter. This led to beneficial results in the area. The level of education was raised, health care was improved and it was due to Spanish influence that Lecce became the centre of that extraordinary revival in architecture which we call the southern Baroque of Lecce. In the last century the palace was acquired by the d'Aspe family, the maternal ancestors of the present owners.

The original Palazzo dei Conti di Lecce was probably erected over the ruins of the Roman fortress during the period of Norman occupation (1060-1200). The city flourished under the d'Enghiens. The first half of the fifteenth century was a period of peace and prosperity. It was almost certainly during that period that the palace was rebuilt and redecorated. The property changed hands several times before passing to the dei Morisco family from Capua in 1700. It was during the period of their ownership in the eighteenth century that the palace acquired the appearance which it has today. During the great epoch of Lecce Baroque, they commissioned their architect Emanuele Manieri, the son of Mauro Manieri

ABOVE: *Detail of a door panel in the music room by an unknown eighteenth-century artist.*

RIGHT: *The music room with its Bösendorfer concert grand of 1850 and eclectic furnishings, including two paintings on either side of the door by the English artists John Heils (left) and Joseph Highmore (right).*

(who designed the façade of the cathedral), to build the grand staircase and the internal façade of their palazzo.

The courtyard, although not as ornate in its facings as some of the church façades, is a good example of the lavish decoration applied by the architects of the Golden Age of Lecce's Baroque to the outer walls of their buildings. The interiors are spacious and elegant. The music room is interesting with its Bösendorfer concert grand piano of 1850, pictures on either side of the doorway of the Countess of Rochester and Lady Sutherland, fine Bohemian chandelier, modern Persian carpet and modern replicas of Italian eighteenth-century furniture. The door panels with the eighteenth-century paintings of musicians are charming. There is also a fine library. In a city as cultivated as Lecce, a palazzo without a library and a music room would seem to be an anomaly. The dining room is impressive with its vaulted ceiling. The massive teak dinner table and sideboard were made from the timbers of a nineteenth-century sailing ship. This palace is a fine example of the historical associations and refined culture of Lecce.

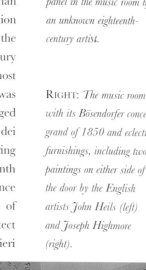

ABOVE: *The library has comfortable chairs and sofas and well-stocked shelves.*

ABOVE: *The dining room, with table and sideboard made from the timbers of a sailing ship. The wall sconces over the sideboard date from the early eighteenth century.*

PALAZZO BISCARI
Catania, Sicily

Stretched out between the Via Museo Biscari to the north and the Via Dusmet to the south in the town of Catania on the eastern shore of Sicily is the most imposing of the city's private dwellings, the enormous Palazzo Biscari. Catania is now a pleasant and lively town with some of the best shops in Italy and a fine opera house to commemorate one of its illustrious sons, the composer Vincenzo Bellini (1801–35). The town was almost entirely destroyed by a devastating earthquake in 1693. The Catanians, however, whose history reaches back to a Greek settlement from Naxos founded in c.729 BC, have through the ages shown a remarkable capacity for survival and it did not take them more than a few decades to rebuild their city. This was achieved under the guidance of the capable and energetic architect-priest from Palermo, G. B. Vaccarini, who trained as an architect in Rome where he was influenced by the great Baroque builders and especially by Borromini.

LEFT: *The south side of the courtyard at the front of the palace. The width of the approach and the contrast between the black lava-stone of the steps and walls and the white Syracuse stone of the portal, window frames and balustrades make this a very striking entrance.*

Two other architects also played an important role in the reconstruction of their native city of Catania and shared in the rebuilding of its most notable church, San Nicolò (1735), the largest of the Sicilian churches. These were Antonino Amato, the elder of the two, and Francesco Battaglia. The former also began to work on the renewal of the Paternò family property which stood on the sixteenth-century bastions of the city built during the reign of the Emperor Charles V.

The Paternò family had played an important role in Sicily's history since the eleventh century, contributing illustrious leaders of Church and state in the conduct of the island's affairs. They

LEFT: *The first-floor terrace of the south front is a marvel of unsophisticated and sculpture, imbued with an irresistible exuberance.*

exercised special influence in Catania. Ignazio Paternò Castello was the sixth Prince of Biscari and it was he above all who was responsible for the unique palazzo which we see today. The first work for the reconstruction of the palace began in 1695 but the actual building of it seems to have begun only after May 1702 when Antonino Amato was the architect in charge, perhaps working to designs by Alonzo Di Benedetto. After this first phase the work went forward (1740–80) under the direction of Francesco Battaglia stimulated by the ideas of his employer, the Prince of Biscari, who was a widely read and much travelled man. This collaboration led to the building of one of the most remarkable palaces in Sicily, a masterpiece of the Rococo inside while the outside, as Sacheverell Sitwell has observed, shows the influence of the Churrigueresque manner also.

LEFT: *A room in the Quarto di Villeggiatura, a section of the palazzo built to provide good light and ventilation.*

ABOVE: *A detail of the decoration in the Galleria degli Ucelli ('birds').*

ABOVE: *Detail of the ceiling of the Gran Salone frescoed by Sebastiano del Monaco.*

RIGHT: *The Galleria degli Ucelli, a large living room in which chiefly the decoration consists largely of bird paintings, executed, it is supposed, by Sebastiano del Monaco who was commissioned to do the main fresco work in the palace.*

The most striking external views of the palazzo are obtained on the south side from Via Dusmet, where the remarkable framing of the windows looking onto the terrace, with the friskily frolicking putti over the tympanum and the telamons on the jambs, is brilliantly highlighted in the white stone of Syracuse against the dark lava-dust wash of the walls. In the spacious courtyard a double flight of black lava-stone steps with white balustrades leads up to a large white-framed main doorway under a white arch placed against the dark background of the wall, providing a wonderful setting for a grand entry.

There is a special suite called Il Quarto di Villeggiatura (the holiday quarters), which is an apartment of particularly light and well-ventilated rooms giving onto a wide terrace used in spring and summer weather. To go into *villeggiatura* is the Italian phrase for escaping from summer heat in the towns to the fresh breezes of the seaside or the countryside.

The interior decoration of rooms on the *piano nobile* is varied but effective, and was carried out by the painter Sebastiano del Monaco with the assistance, for the stucco work, of Gioiacchino Gianforma and Ignazio Mazzeo. The painting of the Galleria degli Uccelli, with highly coloured exotic birds, is particularly notable. Altogether the decoration of the reception rooms in the Palazzo Biscari represents a work of Rococo artistry different from the recognised masterpieces in northern Europe but without doubt of a very high standard.

A PALAZZETTO IN VENICE

hough some of the palaces along the Grand Canal in Venice were built as early as the thirteenth century the great period of palace building was from the fifteenth to the end of the eighteenth centuries. The older palaces like the Palazzo Loredan and the Palazzo Farsetti, on the straight middle reach of the canal, are in the pre-Gothic Veneto-Byzantine style. They introduce us, however, to a feature of Venetian palace building which has maintained a high degree of constancy in later ages and reminds us that these aristocratic buildings were erected by merchants for the purpose of trade. The main feature of these palaces is the ground floor portico for loading and unloading merchandise, leading into a large hall called the *androne*, which was used for the conduct of business. Upstairs were the living rooms, beginning with a substantial *salone* over the *androne*, while the bedrooms were behind or on an upper floor. At the rear of the house was a courtyard with a well and an open staircase, the latter being accommodated later on within the building.

One of the most famous of the small palaces, the Ca' d'Oro (1420–34), was built by Marino Contarini, a member of a leading Venetian family. It presented such an outburst of lavish display and opulence, such intricacies of tracery by the best Lombard and Venetian stone-carvers, such splashes of gilt alternating with cinnabar red and ultramarine blue that even the Venetians must have been amazed. Now the gilt and pigment have been worn away by the weather, but enough palaces had already been built on the banks of the 3,800-metre (4,150-yard)-long Grand Canal by the beginning of the sixteenth century not merely to amaze Venetians but to astound foreigners. 'A cytie glorious . . . above all places yt ever I sawe,' wrote an English cleric in 1505, echoing a French ambassador who ten years earlier described it as '*la plus triumphante cite que j'aye jamais veue*'. He was most startled to see a 600-ton galley riding at anchor in front of one of the palaces.

The Renaissance brought a different kind of beauty to the banks of the canal with the Palazzo Vendramin-Calergi (completed 1509) by the great architect Mauro Codussi from Bergamo. This was the first palace in which the façade was moulded throughout by the classical order of three superimposed levels of Corinthian columns.

LEFT: *A palazzetto overlooking the Grand Canal.*

OPPOSITE: *A living room, with a large painted period cupboard and stucco decoration on the ceiling.*

Successive centuries saw the appearance of ever more imposing palaces, one of the last and largest being the Palazzo Rezzonico near the Accademia Bridge.

The palace is now a museum with a very interesting collection of Venetian furnishings of the eighteenth century when there was a craze for lacquered furniture and chinoiserie decoration. It must not be imagined, however, that Venetian families used their showy salons for any but the greatest occasions as when they entertained a foreign ambassador or potentate. Nor would the larger palaces, in spite of a horde of servants who were accommodated on the top floor, be occupied only by the head of the family. A numerous progeny would enjoy hospitality there as well. Later it became usual to create apartments in these large buildings for selling or leasing, and this is the case today when a house owner or tenant is able to enjoy the amenities of living in a palazzo without being a millionaire.

Such apartments are usually spacious, with a large entrance hall, several drawing rooms with at least one overlooking the canal, a large dining room and several bedrooms, sometimes with elaborate four-poster beds. Rooms may be designated by a special feature – the dominant colour, the pictures, the decoration, the mirrors or an historical association like the Doge's Bedroom. But whatever the variety of nomenclature, the standard of taste and comfort is invariably high.

The photographs illustrate an example of a medium-sized apartment in one of the palaces on the Grand Canal. The palace is mainly of the late sixteenth century but the interior decoration and the furniture is mostly of the seventeenth and eighteenth centuries. The large cupboard in the drawing room is Venetian, an important period piece. The tiled fireplace in another drawing room is seventeenth century. Another larger living room with family portraits on the walls contains attractive furniture mainly of the eighteenth century. The large bedroom with striking wallpaper and a Venetian glass headboard is known as the Doge's Bedroom, the Doge being Alvise Pisani (1735–41), who had been Venetian ambassador to the Court of Queen Anne. The mirror, furniture and ceiling decoration are of the eighteenth century. In the dining room the chandelier is eighteenth-century Murano glass made in imitation of the Austrian chandeliers of the period. The tablecloth is a very fine reproduction of a seventeenth-century patterned cloth made by a firm near Como.

This apartment displays the elegance and comfort which remain a feature of many of the apartments in the palaces of Venice to this day.

ABOVE: *The Doge's Bedroom, with eighteenth-century furniture and an impressive gilt and glass headboard.*

LEFT: *Another living room, with mostly eighteenth-century furniture and portraits on the wall of some of the wives who married into the family.*

ABOVE: *The main staircase, with a finely decorated barrel vault.*

A PALAZZO IN CENTRAL ROME

LEFT: *The drawing room has a fine coffered ceiling (c.1660), predominantly eighteenth-century furniture and a mirror over the fireplace with a gilded bronze 'Gloria' frame.*

The principal area for the palaces of Rome is in the horn of the Tiber's left bank, from the modern Ponte Cavour to the ancient bridges of Cestio and Fabricio, which join the Tiber's only island to its shores. The great age of the Roman palaces was from the Early Renaissance in Rome beginning with the Palazzo Venezia (1467) to the Palazzo Braschi built in the last decade of the eighteenth century – though in the Renaissance manner, and even then a fine building. This is more than can be said for the huge, dull Palazzo Brancaccio built just about a hundred years later.

Many of the 120 or so palaces in Rome have been bought by public or private institutions. Some have been secured to house foreign embassies. The best choice was made by the French when they acquired the Palazzo Farnese. Most have been subdivided into a number of apartments or offices, large and small. In the nineteenth century they were still often family homes providing a residence for several generations of one family.

The main features of a Roman palazzo are the façade, often added on to an older building, so that a Renaissance palazzo might have a Baroque or Rococo front; one or more spacious courtyards with fountains and an open arcade on the ground level; and a grand staircase which, following Palladio's advice is 'clear, ample and commodious to ascend, inviting, as it were, people to go up'. This was achieved by using broad, shallow steps. The next floor is the *piano nobile*, or main floor, containing suites of fine, large rooms including a ballroom, a music room, a library and various salons and, of course, a large dining room. On the upper floors there is a series of apartments with bedrooms and living rooms; these are now very often converted into flats.

A notable feature of the Roman palazzo is the terrace or roof garden. There may be several of these in one palazzo, since the Roman palace has a roving roof of many half-hidden crannies at different levels; and whenever possible a roof garden will be catching the sun's rays at the meridian. These soaring gardens constitute one of the great pleasures of living in a palazzo, for you

LEFT: *The furniture in the entrance hall of this palazzo apartment includes two Empire-style pieces: a large mirror with a carved gilt wooden frame and below this a wide console, also of gilded wood, with a marble top.*

ABOVE: *A corner of one of the bedrooms, which was designed by an architect who was a tenant in the apartment in the 1930s.*

The terrace garden on one of the upper storeys. The plants often found on such terraces are small citrus fruit trees, sweet smelling and other geraniums, plumbago, roses and wisteria.

will often be assured of a wonderful view and, at most times of the year, of an alfresco meal under a wide-spreading umbrella with the fashionable white-painted furniture on terracotta paving tiles. There you will be surrounded by diverse orange, lemon and bergamot trees in large earthenware pots. You will be safeguarded from a fall into the courtyard or street by a wrought-iron balustrade. A variety of colourful flowers in terracotta boxes will refresh your eyes. You will breathe a much fresher air than in the streets, and there will be a semblance of silence compared with the hubbub below.

In the example of a palazzo apartment portrayed here, the interior decoration is somewhat eclectic. The pleasant vaulted entrance hall contains a fine Empire console over which hangs a large mirror also of the same period. The large drawing room has a beamed and coffered ceiling with painted decoration of about the time when this wing of the palazzo was completed (c.1660). The furniture is mostly eighteenth century, with a large modern sofa to provide extra comfort. There is a striking mirror over the fireplace with a gilded bronze frame of the type called Gloria, with cherubs' heads floating among clouds. One of the bedrooms strikes a different note from the rooms described above. It is modern, designed by an architect who occupied the apartment in the early thirties and unadorned except for bands of white marking the undulating articulation of the grey walls and ceiling which form alcoves and vaults.

And finally there is a terrace. The view from here is of the tower of a Baroque church and, some way off across the many russet-coloured, tiled roofs, another terrace and another garden on the roof of another palazzo.

CASTELLO DI MONTICELLO D'ALBA
Piedmont

The castle is situated in the Langhe region of Piedmont on a hillock near the small town of Monticello d'Alba some kilometres west of Alba itself. The scenery round about is varied – a countryside scattered with vineyards, fields of wheat, hillocks and castles.

Like the Valle d'Aosta running north towards Mont Blanc, the region of Langhe, stretching

south of Turin to Cuneo, is a land of many castles. After the collapse of the Roman Empire in the fifth century it was fought over by successive invaders – Ostrogoths, Burgundians, Byzantines, Goths, Lombards and Franks. It was later taken over by feudal lords who attempted to control their domains by building castles at all serviceable points of vantage like river crossings and mountain passes. The castles were sited to obtain a good view of approaching enemies, who might be Saracen pirates moving inland to plunder – in 892 they sacked and destroyed Alba – or Hungarian cavalry galloping in from the eastern plains. When not under attack by foreign invaders, the local counts found a use for their castles by waging war on one another. Out of these feuds there emerged

RIGHT: *The Galleria, a main living room, with unusual mural decoration and late eighteenth-century furniture.*

ABOVE: *The courtyard of the castle, which was built about 1350, includes both Romanesque and Gothic window arches.*

RIGHT: *The imposing exterior, showing the different-shaped towers and the apertures towards the top of the walls through which boulders could be flung onto attackers below.*

three dominant overlords, the Dukes of Savoy and the Marquises of Saluzzo and of Monferrato.

It is claimed that the castle of Monticello d'Alba may have been founded as early as the tenth century but the oldest parts of the building we see today date from the second half of the fourteenth century when the castle came into the hands of the Roero family who are the owners of it to this day. Though extensively overhauled in the late 1300s, the castle has retained its appearance of a major fortress of the High Middle Ages.

Inside the castle walls there is a fine fourteenth-century courtyard, brick built with a cobbled pavement and an arcade of Gothic arches.

A good deal of interior decoration was carried out in the late eighteenth century to match the taste of the times and it was then that the drawbridge was removed and a new garden layout was added. Inside the building itself the vaulted Galleria has elaborate eighteenth-century wall decoration, with the paintings of dead game and unclothed statuesque human figures in *trompe-l'oeil* aedicules, or niches, at either end, and elegant period furniture. Another large room called La Sala degli Stemmi, also with a vaulted ceiling and a fine hooded fireplace (a common feature in Piedmontese castles), justifies its name with a display of the coats of arms of successive Roero countesses.

Returning to the outside of the castle, which looks very impressive, there is one most unusual feature to note. It has three towers of different shapes – one round, one square and the other octagonal. Whether this improved its defensive efficiency is hard to say but it is aesthetically intriguing. The medieval character of the building has been very well preserved thanks to the lavish care bestowed upon it by the owners.

LEFT: *The Sala degli Stemmi ('shields') takes its name from the escutcheons over the cornice at the top of the walls bearing the coats of arms of the Roero family countesses.*

ABOVE: *The mural decoration in the Galleria makes use of* trompe l'oeil *technique to emphasize the rather gruesome effect of the statuesque emaciated nudes and hanging game.*

A CASTLE IN PIEDMONT

ABOVE: *Part of the east front of the castle overlooking the garden.*

BELOW: *The Sala delle Vedute, 'room with views', a writing room with a painted frieze showing the castle in the centre.*

The castle stands on a hill in a narrow valley on a site which is first mentioned in imperial deeds of the middle of the twelfth century. In the following century it passed into the hands of a powerful local family which in one or other of its branches has retained it to the present day. The castle is a good example of an ancient fabric which has been well preserved by numerous restorations both outside and in.

The entrance to the castle precincts is through a turreted medieval gateway giving access to a complex of buildings which were constructed from the twelfth to the nineteenth centuries, although the main body was probably erected in the fifteenth century. Looking along the length of the west front, one is immediately struck by the sight of a tall fourteenth-century tower with splendid Gothic windows surrounded by friezes and elaborate brick cornices. These handsome openings are continued along the front towards the other end, which is a reconstruction from the mid-seventeenth century of a part of the castle that had been demolished a hundred years before in local warfare. To complete this end, another tower was added at the same time, less tall than the earlier one but likewise very impressive. Behind this wing of the castle front there existed a spacious courtyard opening up on one side

ABOVE: *The elegant breakfast room is an eclectic mixture, with moulded ogee arches over the door frames, a round arch for the window, and furniture showing a strong late eighteenth-century English influence.*

towards the park.

Within the walls of these massive buildings a number of fine rooms were contained for domestic use and for entertaining. One particularly striking state room has a coffered ceiling of the fifteenth century and a monumental chimneypiece with very fine stucco decoration. The bedrooms are large and colourful. A writing room has an unusually wide *trompe l'oeil* frescoed frieze between the heavily beamed ceiling and the cornice.

Most of the interior decoration for the living rooms is of the nineteenth or twentieth centuries. By means of skilful selection and a regard for accommodation, these rooms, though surrounded by such heavy masonry, give a pleasing sense of elegance and contentment.

ABOVE: *A reception room, with beams supporting the ceiling, is dominated by a monumental chimneypiece with fine stucco decoration. Family portraits hang on the walls.*

RIGHT: *The four-poster bed and furniture in this bedroom are late eighteenth century. The wallpaper is a copy of a Chinese pattern.*

CASTELLO DI RIVALTA
Emilia-Romagna.

*T*he Castle of Rivalta stands on a spur of the left bank of the River Trebbia as it approaches the Po plain from the defiles of the Apennines a short way south of Piacenza. This magnificent building has belonged to the ancient Landi family since the early fourteenth century. It is probable that some kind of fortress stood on this site from imperial Roman times because the milestone names of small neighbouring townships (Quarto, Settima) strongly suggest the existence of a Roman military road running down the valley to Piacenza.

A document of 1048 affirms the presence of a castle in this place by that date and it was acquired for the Landi family by Obbizzo Landi at the beginning of the fourteenth century. It has remained the property of the Landis to this day. The Landi family are thought to have had their origin in Piacenza where they became prominent as merchants, bankers and civic administrators. By the middle of the thirteenth century they had already acquired extensive properties in the Apennine valleys. Their hold on Rivalta was at times precarious owing to the sporadic enmity of the rulers of Milan and later of the Farnese rulers of Parma and Piacenza, but though the castle was transferred from one branch of the Landi family to another it remained with that dynasty. About the

ABOVE: *The courtyard of the castle, built in the middle of the fifteenth century by Count Manfredo Landi, shows all the refinement of a Renaissance palazzo in town. It was perhaps designed by Antonio da Lugano and executed by his overseer of works Antonio da Pavia.*

RIGHT: *The walls of the Yellow Sitting Room in the south wing are of a rich cream colour reinforced by the wide bands of a golden yellow frame round the pictures. A pleasant contrast is provided by sofas with bright chintz covers.*

LEFT: *The main entrance to the castle was added in the eighteenth century in rather heavy classical style.*

middle of the last century it was inherited by the Zanardi Landi family who are the present owners.

Different parts of the castle are identified with different owners and epochs. The great square tower visible at the entrance of the *borgo*, or village, was completed in 1050 with the surrounding walls. The garden forecourt and the entrance façade are a restoration of the late eighteenth century. The inside courtyard dates from about 1450 and was built by Count Manfredo Landi in the same Early Renaissance style as his contemporary palazzo in Piacenza. Its double row of arcades is very stylish. Behind the south-west corner of the courtyard the top of the tall castle tower is visible. This is a massive round tower probably built at the same time as the courtyard. During an eighteenth-century restoration a high and much slimmer cylindrical extension ending in a small turret capped by a spire was added to the tower. Other new building at this time included the erection of a new grand staircase and a vast apron of wall (1711) on the east side of the castle between the embankment and the river. An enlargement of the garden was carried out the same time.

A great change was effected by Count Giuseppe Landi with the completion in 1780 of an entire redecoration of the living rooms inside the castle. Three of these are especially noteworthy. The dining room was enlivened with a wall decoration of blue and white dishes, called 'Compagnia delle Indie', which were flooding into Europe from the Far East. The furniture was mainly Neoclassical. The billiard room was decorated by a fine ceiling fresco and wall paintings (1789) of rustic scenes, the former by Paolo Borroni from Voghera and the latter by a gifted Lombard decorator, Filippo Comerio. The paintings and furniture in light shades give added prominence to the green baize on the billiard table. The kitchen with its array of copper ware and its antlers on the walls is also a striking room which was in use from 1800 to 1940.

A large room was furnished in the Neoclassical style to provide this dining room. The pictures are late eighteenth-century landscapes, and the fine collection of blue and white Chinese dishes was a product of the trade carried on by the East India Companies from Canton and other ports in China, which became intense in the eighteenth century.

LEFT: *The music room displays a pleasing variety of decoration.*

RIGHT: *This kitchen was fitted into an outhouse in the early nineteenth century and remained in use until 1940. It contains a splendid display of copper kitchenware.*

LEFT: *A corner of a small first-floor sitting room, which demonstrates that not only the larger rooms in the castle are ornately decorated.*

RIGHT: *The billiard room is one of the best decorated rooms in the castle, with wall frescoes of rustic scenes by Filippo Comerio, dated 1789, and a ceiling fresco (1771) by Paolo Borroni of Voghera.*

ABBAZIA DI PRAGLIA
Veneto

The Benedictine monastery and church of Praglia are situated in an area of lush meadows at the foot of the Euganean hills some kilometres west of Padua. The monastery was founded as an independent community in 1304. The community grew rapidly from the last decade of the fifteenth century when the present monastery and church were erected to the designs of the famous Lombard architect resident in Venice, Tullio Soleri, known as Tullio Lombardo.

The Benedictines were the earliest monastic foundation in Italy having started under the guidance of St Benedict of Nursia with his monastery at Subiaco in the mountains east of Rome. In about 529 he founded Monte Cassino where he established a congregation which was to become famous as a source of culture and a mainspring of European civilisation. He achieved this result by writing a constitution for his order by which every Benedictine monastery has been ruled to this day. This provides for the independence of each community under a single elected abbot, the monks dividing their time between prayer, manual labour and study. The

LEFT: *A fifteenth-century cloister at Praglia, which like some Venetian palaces mixes both classical and Gothic styles.*

RIGHT: *The Sala degli Stucci is reserved for the entertainment of guests and is distinguished by its beautiful stucco decoration.*

BELOW LEFT: *A general view of the monastery buildings, which were mostly begun in the late fifteenth century in a reconstruction of plans by Tullio Lombardo.*

monasteries became great centres for the propagation of the Christian faith, for the preservation of ancient classical culture and for the promotion of agriculture and good husbandry. They were usually sited in rather remote and peaceful places. Such a place was Praglia, though with the passing of time its remoteness has diminished. Yet it remains a beautiful and unspoiled location.

Tullio Lombardo belonged to one of the various groups of stonemasons, highly skilled as sculptors and architects, who migrated from their homeland around Lake Lugano to find work in other parts of Italy or abroad. The group which settled in Venice, led by Tullio's father Pietro, was instrumental in conducting the transition which led Venetian architecture from the Gothic to the Early Renaissance style.

Tullio Lombardo's church at Praglia and the attached monastery (1490-1548) are Renaissance buildings of some distinction. At the centre of the monastery is the Chiostro Pensile, or Hanging

Cloister, so called because it is at first-floor level. It is surrounded by a fine arcade with columns of white Istrian stone and it has an elegant carved and canopied well-head in the middle of the square. The monks' rooms open onto the cloister. In another part of the monastery is the guests' reception room with remarkably fine stucco decoration above the doors.

The art of stucco decoration was given a great impetus after the discovery (*c*.1500) of some remarkably fine decorative features, described by Vasari as 'little grotesques, small figures and scenes with other ornaments of stucco in low relief,' in underground chambers in the ruins of Nero's Domus Aurea near the Colosseum in Rome. One of Raphael's pupils, Giovanni da Udine, was inspired by the fine quality of these grotesques to make experiments (using marble dust in the place of pozzolana with white lime of travertine) to procure a paste for stucco as good as, if not better than, that of the Romans in imperial times. With his new found skill and in association with Raphael he decorated the Loggias in the Vatican. His decorative style soon spread throughout Italy and abroad. It would have penetrated into his native Veneto in time to influence the artists who produced the stuccos in the Praglia monastery. Benedictine hospitality is renowned, but I doubt whether many monastic reception rooms could regale visitors, awaiting the arrival of the guest-master, with such fine examples of stucco work.

Behind the monastery there is a spacious walled garden with vines and vegetables. This too is very much in the Benedictine tradition.

ABOVE RIGHT: *The Sala degli Abbati is used as a small dining room or reception room.*

RIGHT: *This cloister, one of three in the monastery, has an elegant well-head in the centre and a good view of the campanile.*

A corridor near the central
courtyard, which has a
cross-vaulted ceiling, a
marble floor and a frescoed
tympanum over the doorway.

A VILLA NEAR SALERNO
Campania

The villa is situated in the hilly country between Mount Vesuvius and Salerno. Like other Vesuvian villas built as summer residences for dwellers in neighbouring towns, it has a garden and spectacular views, and benefits from a cooler atmosphere than that of the cities. The garden lies between the front gate onto the road and the house itself and is not very large. Its design was, however, influenced by that of the English garden of the Royal Palace of Caserta near Naples, and it is noted for its splendid camellias.

The villa was built in the late eighteenth century, and a wing was added early in the nineteenth century. The front entrance with a fine portico leads into a hallway where one's attention is immediately attracted by a large majolica ewer on a cylindrical base, a reminder of the importance of ceramicware in Neapolitan décor. As one goes from room to room, one is

increasingly aware of this feature, with tiled floors in the dining room and in the so-called Swiss Room. Some of the ceilings are decorated with frescoes, as in the Pompeiian room. One bedroom contains various contrasting elements: a very light floor and ceiling, brightly coloured and patterned walls and a plain brass bedstead. The dining room is very attractive: the rather heavy mahogany furniture sets off the lightly decorated ceiling and plain walls where an unusual amount of room is provided for the single large painting on each wall space.

The villa and its garden present a very agreeable refuge from the oppressive summer heat and stress of the cities – a beautiful environment and premises arranged for comfortable living.

ABOVE: *The dining room makes an attractive ensemble with tiled floor, mahogany furniture, plain peach-coloured walls, and well-hung paintings by a local artist.*

ABOVE: *A bedroom with simple brass bedsteads, somewhat exuberant floral decoration on the walls and painted door panels.*

LEFT: *The house was built in Neoclassical style in the late eighteenth century with a wing added in the following century.*

ABOVE: *Detail of the Swiss Room's tiled floor, one of several tiled pavements in the house.*

LEFT: *The entrance hall is a stylish room with a prominent 'Vecchia Napoli' ceramic ewer, a tiled pavement and a vaulted and frescoed ceiling.*

BELOW: *The delightful garden has some rare trees and shrubs.*

VILLA CICOGNA MOZZONI
Lombardy

*S*ituated between Porto Ceresio on Lake Lugano and Varese in a valley running northwards towards the lake, the mainly sixteenth-century Villa Cicogna Mozzoni is reached from the main road up a long avenue of trees which emerges on the piazza in front of the house and its fine portal. The villa has been the property of the family for over 500 years. The two branches of the family merged in 1584 when Donna Angela Mozzoni, whose portrait hangs in the house, married Count Giovanni Pietro II of the Cicogna family, bringing the villa to their joint property as part of her dowry. The Mozzoni family were landowners in the neighbourhood.

The Cicogna family appears prominently in the histories both of Milan and of Venice. From the fourteenth century members of the family were chosen as counsellors of the Dukes of Milan. In 1529 Giovanni Pietro Cicogna conquered an invading French army at Landriano near Milan while in the service of the Emperor Charles V, who made him a count and conferred on him the right to emblazon the imperial eagle on his coat of arms. In 1585 Pasquale Cicogna was Doge of Venice and played an important diplomatic role in supporting Henry IV as King of France. The famous Rialto Bridge was built in Venice during his reign. Thereafter, Cicognas continued to play a prominent part in the service of Milan and her rulers, including the Emperors of Austria and France.

The fifteenth-century hunting lodge, which

RIGHT: An arcaded wing of the villa erected between 1550 and 1570, with part of a formal garden in the foreground.

LEFT: Detail of a fresco in the west-side loggia showing examples of foliage and fruit to be found in the garden as well as flying nymphs in the pendentives.

RIGHT: The loggia on the west side of the courtyard, with frescoes by the Campi brothers of Cremona, who carried out most of the decoration in the villa.

The grand staircase is also decorated with frescoes: views of Lake Lugano and the surrounding hills on the walls, and floral and geometric themes, as well as cherubs, festoons and the coat of arms, on the ceiling. The colour of these frescoes has been particularly well preserved.

constitutes the earliest part of the building, was enlarged in the following century to create a classic example of a Lombard Renaissance villa by the addition of two wings to form a central court leading to a garden. An interesting feature of this villa is its exemplification of Renaissance ideas about the relationship of the building to its environment, into which the villa, its gardens and its park are all skilfully integrated. A main feature of the garden is the water-staircase flanked by cypresses, which is typical of the Roman Renaissance. This rises from the great terrace along the west side of the villa to the woodland on the hillside above.

The central courtyard is flanked by the two wings mentioned above. The ground floor of these wings is formed by two loggias, while for the central section a painted loggia was contrived along the wall. The two authentic loggias and many of the rooms are frescoed on walls and ceilings, the painters being two pupils of Giulio Romano, the Campi brothers from Cremona. Thematically, the frescoes consist of *trompe l'oeil* pergolas with swags of fruit, flowers and vegetables and some early grotesques.

A grand staircase, its walls finely frescoed with

ABOVE: *Detail of a painted frieze between the cornice and the ceiling in one of the bedrooms, showing mythological and grotesque motifs.*

views of Lake Lugano and its surrounding hills, leads to the *piano nobile* and the main living rooms of the house, which look onto a long, gravelled terrace and the water-staircase previously mentioned. Among these rooms is the impressive main salon with a big fireplace showing Mars and Venus on the hood. A wide frieze around the top of the walls, on which hang ancestral portraits, represents an abundance of fruits from the orchards, and vegetables and flowers from the gardens.

Another fine room is the library once used as a chapel. Here another large fireplace is predominant, occupying most of the end wall with Venus once again portrayed on the hood of the fireplace, in this case with Vulcan. Other frescoes

ABOVE: *The library is one of the most elegant rooms on the first floor, rectangular in shape and with a fine fireplace, on the hood of which is a fresco of Venus and Vulcan.*

on the walls portray Apollo and the Muses. Two items of furniture here are of considerable interest, a bride's dowry trunk in wrought iron with studs and a rounded lid, and a reading table, rather higher than was usual at the time, dating from 1670. Most rooms overlook the gardens. Some of the older interiors have coffered wooden ceilings painted in different colours.

The owners of this elegant villa, although no longer resident there, still supervise the careful maintenance which has kept it in such an excellent state of repair.

VILLA PISANI
Bagnolo

The urge to go to the countryside on terra firma was an old obsession among the inhabitants of Venice. At first it could only be indulged by the owners of castles within the narrow limits of the Venetian mainland. But after Venice had enlarged her territory in the middle of the fifteenth century from Trent to the Po and from the Adda to the Isonzo River and to Istria, the number of city dwellers with country retreats grew rapidly. By 1520 it became a steady stream – first to castles which could be safely converted to villas, then to the villas built entirely for leisure and pleasure, if possible with water alongside. A favourite site would be on a canal like the Brenta perhaps, or on some slope of the Euganean hills.

The best architects were called in to lay out these new villas with their sumptuous gardens,

Michele Sanmicheli and Jacopo Sansovino among others, but more especially Andrea Palladio, the greatest of them all. The villas were used quite often for learned gatherings of poets, scholars, musicians and high churchmen, all humanists dedicated to the discussion of philosophy and a new interpretation of the classics. But as time went on, new generations of architects added their handiwork to that of the earlier masters, with the names of Scamozzi, Longhena, Preti, Muttoni and Massari supplanting those of Palladio and Sansovino with ever larger mansions. The intellectual gatherings gave way to theatre shows and festivities, and in the eighteenth century, as a fitting backcloth to all this human elegance, frescoed figures by Giovanni Battista and Gian Domenico Tiepolo stared down from walls and

RIGHT: *One of the living rooms, which is relatively unadorned but very comfortable looking, with modern furniture and a simple chimneypiece and door frame.*

LEFT: *The south front of the villa, which was one of the first designed by Palladio and was built about 1544 for the Pisani family.*

ceilings on to the feasting crowds below.

The Brenta Canal, which joined the lagoon of Venice to Padua, was a favourite passage for Venetians going to their houses on the mainland and became the site of so many of the most beautiful of the villas of the Veneto that it was known as the Riviera of the Brenta. Nevertheless, much as the Venetian liked to escape to the greenery and variety and rural amenities of his country villa whether on the canal, in the foothills of the Alps, on the slopes of the Euganean hills or at Lonigo, his heart remained attached to his palazzo in Venice. This may explain why so many of the villas fell into decay and shows how praiseworthy are the endeavours of those owners who maintain their heritage in a good state of repair.

The Villa Pisani at Bagnolo near Lonigo is one of the earliest villas built by Palladio within a few

years after his first visit to Rome in 1541. It was commissioned by Counts Vittore, Daniele and Mauro Pisani of Venice. The work was completed in 1544 without the plan having been carried out fully. Moreover, the part which had been constructed was badly damaged by fire in 1806 and by bombardment during World War II. What has since been reconstructed is the west wing, which has a prominently rusticated classical front flanked by two short towers.

The use of rustication in architecture was practised by the ancient Romans, such as on the Porta Maggiore in Rome (AD 52), and was renewed in the Renaissance in the fifteenth and sixteenth centuries, for instance on the Palazzo Strozzi (1489–1523) in Florence, 'the rusticated palazzo par excellence'. Rustication was thought to give an appearance of strength to a building. In Venice it was used for the Mint. Its Mannerist look

ABOVE: *Detail of the fresco in the music room.*

must have appealed particularly to Giulio Romano when he built the Palazzo del Tè in Mantua for Federico II Gonzaga (1525–43), and it is thought that this famous building may have influenced Palladio in the 1540s when he was designing country villas for the merchant leaders of Venice.

There are a number of interesting rooms and decorative frescoes in the interior of the villa. Unfortunately the name of the artist who painted the latter, some of which are in the central salon, has not been preserved. One item in the big kitchen, or Cucinone, is of special interest: a simple rectangular hand-basin encased in a lightly modelled marble frame, which is of Palladian design.

LEFT: *The Cucinone ('big kitchen') has a handbasin and surround designed by Palladio.*

The music room, which
like the central hall
contains sixteenth-century
frescoes of merit by an
unknown artist.

PALAZZINA DI CACCIA DI STUPINIGI
Piedmont

*S*tupinigi is a small village in a fertile plain of meadow and woodland, rich in game, about 11 kilometres (7 miles) south-east of Turin. In April 1729 King Victor Amadeus II of Sardinia, also Duke of Savoy and ruler of Piedmont, commissioned his Sicilian architect Filippo Juvarra to build a royal hunting lodge in that place. The construction and decoration were completed in 1734.

Victor Amadeus came from the ancient dynasty of the Counts and then Dukes of Savoy who in 1563 established their capital in Turin. In the eighteenth century Victor Amadeus was active in promoting not only the political and military might of his small country but also its artistic development and the social standing of the court in Turin. The Palazzina di Caccia of Stupinigi certainly added lustre to his crown.

Filippo Juvarra, the architect of this remarkable building, was born in Messina in Sicily of a well-known family of silversmiths and engravers. While still young, he was sent to Rome to study architecture with Carlo Fontana, who gave him not only a firm grasp of classical and Renaissance styles but also a useful grounding in the rich pastures of Roman Baroque. In 1714 he was presented in Messina to King Victor Amadeus who had obtained the crown of Sicily in the preceding year. The king promptly engaged the thirty-eight-year-old Juvarra as his court architect. In this capacity Juvarra executed a number of important commissions in Turin and in Piedmont, chief among which was the grand Basilica of Superga superbly situated on one of the hills behind the city. In 1735 Juvarra transferred to the service of King Philip V of Spain. He designed the

LEFT: *The Salone Centrale provides the most magnificent mingling of late Baroque and early Rococo architecture in Italy.*

RIGHT: *The Sala delle Prospettive ('Hall of Perspectives'), with frescoes of architectural features and landscapes by G. B. Alberoni (1702-84) from Bologna.*

The chapel of St Hubert, with a painting over the altar by the Turinese painter Vittorio Amadeo Rapous (1728-1800), and a fresco in the vault by G. B. Crosato of Venice.

plans for the new royal palace in Madrid. A year later he died there.

In striking contrast to the restrained Baroque features of the Basilica of Superga, the slightly later hunting lodge of Stupinigi displays an altogether astonishing Rococo effervescence, with all the mutability of a succession of stage settings in the theatre. Juvarra was well qualified, after long practice in producing theatrical designs, to create a building for the entertainment of his monarch. His travels in Italy combined with his previous fifteen years of service at the court in Turin enabled him to assemble a team of artists and highly skilled local craftsmen to carry out his plans.

Juvarra's hunting lodge consists of a central building covered by a copper dome, with gabled windows, surmounted by Francesco Ladatte's commanding sculpture of a large stag. This central building is round with four emerging arms, two short wings at the rear and two longer ones on either side of the front.

The focal point of the whole complex is the Salone Centrale, a magnificent ballroom, elliptical in shape, at the centre of the main building. Juvarra's design for the Salone Centrale is an example of décor at its best, remarkable for the restless intricacy of its patterns and for its harmony. A great central dome frescoed by the Valeriani brothers of Venice is supported by fluted columns arranged in an ellipse and surrounded by four wide apses, all connected by a continuous gallery whose curving lines, traced by an elegant balustrade, were lighted by the bracket lamps along the frieze below. The wealth of detail is astonishing: frescoes, corbels, friezes, volutes, mouldings and draperies are everywhere.

Among the examples of craftsmanship exhibited in Stupinigi one can see the work of two of the best Italian cabinet-makers of the eighteenth century: the Roman Pietro Piffetti, a genius of intarsia work and the Piedmontese Mario Bonzanigo, a younger man who was active when the taste for Baroque and Rococo was yielding to the Neoclassical enthusiasm of the early nineteenth century.

ABOVE: *Gilt appliqué on a large mirror in the anteroom of the queen's suite possibly by Giuseppe Mario Bonzanigo, who worked in Stupinigi from 1786 to 1791.*

LEFT: *The winding first-floor gallery of the Salone Centrale and above it the central dome, which the Valeriani brothers frescoed in about six months in 1731.*

ABOVE: *The antechamber of the king's apartment, in whose decoration various artists collaborated, including Bonzanigo, who was responsible for the furniture.*

A TRULLO IN ALBEROBELLO
Apulia

The region of Apulia is one of the flattest and most fertile in Italy, stretching down the Adriatic coast from the great headland of Monte Gargano to the Cape of Leuca in the heel of the peninsula. The wealth of this area has been derived primarily from agriculture: cereals from the Tavoliere (the tableland of Apulia); grapes from around Trani; cherries from Bisceglie; and almonds, olives, quinces, figs, tobacco and vegetables as well as grass for animals. An upland region of the province of Bari, called Le Murge, contains a location beautifully named La Selva di Fasano, in and around the small towns of Alberobello and Locorotondo. This is where the *trulli* are found, over a thousand of them in Alberobello alone. These are round or rectangular houses, covered by conical roofs usually capped by a stone with a ball or a moulded finial on top of it. That is the only decorative feature on the outside of a trullo. The trulli are built of rough ashlar walls whitewashed inside and out. They are spotlessly clean and so are the streets between them in the towns. The limestone rocks of which the trulli are built are found in all the fields round about. The same kind of stones are also used to make walls marking property limits.

The building of a trullo, though requiring considerable skill in laying the stones without mortar in ever-diminishing circular corbelled courses, is a comparatively simple matter and very economical since the stone is everywhere available from the nearby fields and is very close to the surface. The walls of the trulli have to be massive to carry the weight of the high cones. They vary from 1 to 3 metres (3-9 feet) in width. Bedrooms, created out of alcoves set into the walls of the central living room, are hidden from it by a curtain. Entrance apertures are usually formed by

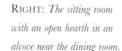

LEFT: *A typical cluster of trulli in Alberobello. White chimneys and finials on the top of the cone-shaped roofs are often prominent features.*

RIGHT: *The sitting room with an open hearth in an alcove near the dining room.*

a rounded archway. If additional rooms were needed, these would be provided by attaching another trullo to the existing one, or more as required. Windows are very small because the daylight in Apulia is normally very strong. The loose structure of the trullo has great advantages. It is like a thermos, containing its inner heat when the weather outside is cold, and maintaining its coolness on the frequently very hot days. It is also resistant to earthquakes and to gales which swirl harmlessly round its aerodynamic curves.

The trulli are nearly all single-storey buildings with a wooden ceiling at a height of about 3 metres (9 feet). Above this, inside the cupola, is an attic for the storage of food or tools though some have recently been converted to bedrooms. In the seventeenth century a rich family built a two-storeyed trullo, but the novelty was not approved of and the Trullo Sovrano, as it was called, survived as a singular, but not very popular, experiment.

The sight of the trulli in Alberobello, and in the green countryside around it, is an entrancing one. But visitors tend to be curious about how they came to be there and nowhere else. What was their origin? This has been much debated. Some historians find their origins in prehistoric Crete or Egypt, others in the Mycaenean *tholoi* or in the Byzantine *torullos*, the cupola-covered room in the imperial palace at Constantinople. In the historical record of Apulia they cannot be traced back beyond the feudal reign in the seventeenth century of the cruel Count of Conversano, Giangirolamo, Acquaviva d'Aragona, who ordered his peasants to build houses without mortar which could be quickly dismantled when the royal inspectors for taxes were due to make a visit. Whatever their origin, the trulli are a unique and outstanding feature in a most attractive landscape which is unique in Italy.

ABOVE: *View from a living area through some characteristic arches to the living room under the cone.*

LEFT: *A ladder leads from the sitting room up to the bedroom in the attic. In many trulli the bedroom is in an alcove off the central room and the attic is used as a storeroom.*

RIGHT: *Many trulli have gardens in front of the house or in a courtyard. In the latter case access is usually from the central room by a low door. Herbs and vegetables are often cultivated as well as flowers.*

CASA COLONICA POGGERINO
Tuscany

The Casa Colonica Poggerino is a converted Tuscan farmhouse in the neighbourhood of Radda in Chianti between Florence and Siena. These farmhouses were often set on a hillock with a good view of the hills and orchards round about and a few cypresses near at hand to give shade in stretches of open country.

The typical layout of some of these farmhouses, which are an eighteenth-century refinement of more primitive farms going back to the Middle Ages and sometimes beyond, consists of a building erected so as to form a courtyard, with the lower floor adapted as required for the storage of agricultural implements and carts, stalls for the cows and draught animals, and perhaps pigsties and a henhouse. The living rooms were on the upper floor, which was reached by an external staircase, at the top of which was a loggia. The central room on this upper storey was a large kitchen with a big fireplace and oven for baking. This served as the main living room and dining room, as well as being a kitchen, and was so much

the heart of the dwelling that the peasants often referred to it as *la casa*, or the house. The outside loggia, sited on the south-facing side of the courtyard and consisting of a long arcade supported by stone pillars, was often used in wet weather as a workroom for the men to mend their baskets and harness and for the women to sew. The bedrooms on the upper floor were reached without passages directly from the kitchen. Most of the older farms embodied a small tower used presumably as a lookout in the early days and later often converted to a pigeon loft and more recently

ABOVE: *The upstairs kitchen and breakfast room next door to the main living room was formerly a washroom.*

LEFT: *The farmhouse from the south, set upon its small hill, or poggerino. The squat tower, which may originally have had a defensive function, is an indication of its age.*

into an additional bedroom.

The Casa Colonica Poggerino differed somewhat from the typical layout described above through having the bread oven located in the courtyard and not in the kitchen. In converting a

working farmhouse to a small residential home, the owners have cleverly adapted the old kitchen as the very elegant main living room with the roof supported on a beamed ceiling and a large hooded fireplace as a principal feature. The comfortable furniture upholstered in chintzes and plain fabrics is modern. The new kitchen-breakfast room has been created next door from a former workroom. The guest bedroom (also on the upper floor) was originally used for cheesemaking.

The character of the lower floor, now a secondary sitting room and kitchen but formerly

ABOVE: *The old kitchen now converted to the main living room. The new and the old mingle very pleasantly here.*

RIGHT: *A corner of the secondary sitting room showing the opening through which hay was originally thrown to the animals.*

used to house sheep and store their hay, has been skilfully preserved by retaining the opening through which the hay was thrown to the animals, and keeping the roughcast appearance of the walls.

AN OLD FARMHOUSE IN TUSCANY

This old farmhouse in the Chianti region of Tuscany is set among hills in a typical Tuscan landscape of vines and olives. The oldest part of the house is the tower which is medieval or earlier, perhaps a thousand years old. The remainder of the farmhouse was added on much later by peasant farmers who incorporated the tower with the later buildings. The main house is on two floors with the living rooms on the upper floor. Down below are the spaces which provide shelter for farm equipment and animals. There was a sheepfold, a pigsty, a henhouse and stalls for draught animals – oxen and horses.

There were no major problems in converting the house about fifteen years ago from a farmhouse to a country residence. The previous owner had four daughters renowned for their

beauty who attracted many admirers to the farm, and he kept a special room for making a very popular *vin santo* for his many guests. Various rooms for the large peasant family provided plenty of living space on the upper floor as well as space for a dining room and kitchen upstairs. A second alfresco dining room was erected on the ground floor for the hot weather, with a downstairs kitchen adjacent to it for light meals.

No structural alterations were needed to adapt the house for its new role. The interior whitewash was retained because it gives the best reflected light indoors from the rather small windows, and also because it is an effective repellent against insects and mites which tend to infest the woodwork in the ceilings unless discouraged. The ceilings are formed of flat tiles supported by wooden beams. The floors are also tiled. Electricity was installed when the present owners bought the house, and they had a mains supply of water to replace the spring and pond which had been the previous source of supply.

The furniture in the living rooms is modern, some of it actually made by the owner. There has been some resourceful adaptation: the pigsty was transformed into an attractive open-air dining room, and the bedposts in the bedrooms were made from the same timber used for the poles in vineyards that support the wires on which the vines are trained.

The conversion of the old farmhouse into a modern residence, with the usual comforts now required, has been carried out most successfully without altering the structure or the appearance of the pleasing old stone building.

RIGHT: *The downstairs sitting room has comfortable modern furnishings and is provided with a good deal of reflective light from the white walls, ceilings and furniture.*

LEFT: *The two-storey farmhouse was built of roughcast stone around an earlier medieval tower.*

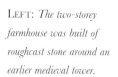

ABOVE: *The upstairs kitchen and dining room is well equipped for the double use for which it was intended.*

LEFT: *The open-air downstairs dining room was cleverly converted from a pigsty. With thatched awning and a lovely view, it is ideal for a cool meal on a hot day.*

ABOVE: *A sparsely furnished upstairs bedroom, with white-washed walls and beamed ceiling.*

GARDENS

ABOVE: *A carved stone flower vase in the garden of a restaurant in Venice.*

LEFT: *The gardens of the Villa Hanbury at La Mortola on the Ligurian riviera are superbly situated on a hillside running down to the sea.*

GARDENS

The contrast which strikes an Englishman immediately when comparing gardens in his own country with those in Italy is one of colour and form. The English garden excels in its display of colour; the Italian in its arrangement of pattern. The most familiar type of Italian garden known to us is that associated with the classical villa or palace of the Renaissance. But this has a long history going back to the last years of the Roman Republic and evolving from the Renaissance to the Baroque garden.

The idea of a pleasure garden, as opposed to a herb or vegetable garden, was unknown to the Romans until the end of the second century BC when Greek culture made a lasting penetration into Roman society. In the latter days of the Roman Republic Lucullus, the millionaire who had introduced cherries and peaches into Italy,

laid out a beautiful garden from his villa, on the site of the present church of Santa Trinità dei Monti, which fell away in terraces down the slope where the Spanish Steps now descend; Cicero had his country retreat in Tusculum, about 16 kilometres (10 miles) south-east of Rome; the writer Varro had an estate and a garden at Cassino; Sallust the historian laid out a famous garden on the Quirinal hill shaped like a hippodrome. Many of the houses in Pompeii had

LEFT: *Semi-tropical vegetation in the garden of the Villa Rufolo.*

gardens and the larger ones contained features which recurred in later Roman gardens and were revived in the gardens of the Renaissance. Such features included the integration of house and garden and the axial planning which enabled you to see the whole length of the garden from the main living room in the house. In some cases this view was prolonged by a *trompe l'oeil* painting on the wall at the end of the garden showing yet another garden with hedges, trees and fountains. This kind of perspective painting was also used to enlarge the sensation of space in courts and colonnades.

The trees and shrubs known to have been planted in the larger Pompeiian gardens were also those to be found later in Renaissance gardens. These included bay trees, oleander, peaches, pomegranates, pears, quinces, cherries and apples. The shrubs commonly used were myrtle, box and laurel. The clipping of hedges for topiary gardening was first carried out by Gaius Matius, the friend of the Emperor Augustus and an expert chef. The flowers grown in the Pompeiian gardens were to some extent the same varieties of roses, lilies and violets which had been grown in Greece, but also included irises, narcissus, crocus, anemones, marigolds, amaranth, gladioli, jasmine

and lavender. Coloured mosaics and statues decorated the shrines and fountains and nympheums of the Pompeiian mansion. Water rippled down staircases into ponds.

A good deal of detailed information about large Roman country gardens is to be found in the descriptions given by Pliny the Younger in two of his letters, probably written between AD 98 and 107 during the reign of the Emperor Trajan. There he describes two of his country houses (the ruins of which can still be seen) with their adjacent gardens at Laurentum on the coast about 25 kilometres (15 miles) south-west of Rome, and Tibernum, now called Città di Castello, in Umbria, whose 'hippodrome' garden was a likely ancestor of the amphitheatre in the Boboli Gardens of Florence. But perhaps the most powerful influence on the Italian Renaissance garden planners was Emperor Hadrian's vast villa

ABOVE LEFT: *Part of the water parterre of the Villa Gamberaia at Settignano near Florence, one of the most beautiful Tuscan gardens.*

ABOVE: *A terrace with lemon trees in large earthenware pots, one of several terraces at the Villa Gamberaia.*

RIGHT: *The eighteenth-century grotto and fountain with tufa stalactites and appliqué pebble decoration at the Villa Gamberaia.*

ABOVE: *The Fontana dell' Ovato in the gardens of the Villa d'Este near Tivoli, designed by Pirro Ligorio in the mid-sixteenth century, is one of the main fountains in a remarkable display of water decoration. The figure of the Sibyl is visible behind the fountain.*

LEFT: *Part of the long row of a hundred fountains at the Villa d'Este, with water jets discharging into two channels at different levels.*

on the plain below Tivoli, already described on p.43. What appears to have impressed Renaissance humanists and planners about Hadrian's Villa was the richness of the décor of mosaics and statues, colonnades and marble revetment; the imaginative use of water in ponds, lakes, cascades and fountains; the coherence of each of the different units forming the parts of the 120-hectare (300-acre) estate even though the whole did not have an overall plan. It would seem also that the idea of landscape gardening on a large scale, if not actually born in the villa's Vale of Tempe, achieved its first clear demonstration there.

The barbarian invasions and the collapse of the Roman Empire in the fifth century put an end temporarily to the construction of large gardens though there is no reason to suppose that small vegetable gardens went out of existence. Moreover the tradition of the enclosed garden as a place of retreat for contemplation survived through to the Middle Ages in the Benedictine monasteries. A rare example of a medieval pleasure garden is, however, the thirteenth-century Villa Rufolo at Ravello.

The acknowledged cradle of the Renaissance garden was Florence where we find that the creation of gardens about the city was always associated with a villa, and the villas were mainly connected with the most prominent members of the Medici family of bankers. In 1457 the founder of that remarkable dynasty, Cosimo the Elder, commissioned his architect Michelozzo Michelozzi to transform an old castellated house at Careggi about 6.5 kilometres (4 miles) north of Florence into a villa with loggias and a garden. It is worth noting that many of the early villas were converted castles or castellated country houses, whose defences were deemed to have become superfluous. The garden at Careggi followed the model of a classical garden using box, bays, cypress, myrtle, scented herbs, pomegranates and quinces, but there were new elements: carnations among the flowers, and oranges and lemons among the fruits, all of which only reached Europe during the Crusades.

Other notable Medicean gardens in the neighbourhood of Florence are the Villa Il Trebbio at Cafaggiolo (another battlemented house converted into a villa in 1451 with the garden added after 1464) and the Villa Medici at Fiesole, where Lorenzo the Magnificent entertained his group of intellectual friends. During the following century the largest and most famous of the Medicean gardens was laid out on the perimeter of the city itself. The Boboli Gardens

occupy the slope between the Pitti palace and the river. They were designed by the Florentine sculptor Niccolò Pericoli Tribolo in 1549 (while he was still working on a Medici villa at Castello) and begun the following year, during which Tribolo died. The work went on well into the next century under Ammanati, Buontalenti and others, with its variety of plantations moving with the times from a Tuscan to a Roman conception of grand garden design.

The most beautiful of the gardens near Florence, which typifies the evolving perception of Tuscan gardening design from the seventeenth to the nineteenth centuries, is the Villa Gamberaia at Settignano. Originally the property of two stonemason brothers Giovanni and Bernardo Gambarelli, who achieved fame as architects under the name of Rosselino, it was sold to successive owners who enlarged it. In 1717 it became the property of the illustrious Capponi family who made the principal alterations which

ABOVE: *The Renaissance garden of the Villa Lante near Viterbo, laid out by Vignola in the sixteenth century, has been acclaimed as the most perfect in Italy.*

account for the garden's present appearance. Among the outstanding features are the water parterre; the grotto, with its decoration of pebble appliqué combined with stucco and tufa stalactites; the lemon terrace; and the bowling avenue. From the Early Renaissance style of the Medici villas the Villa Gamberaia moved during the course of its development into Baroque decoration with statues and grottos.

In Rome the High Renaissance was accompanied by a creative flourish of grand villas and gardens. As in architecture these varied from the strictly classical, like Bramante's Belvedere courtyard and garden of the early years of the sixteenth century, to Pirro Ligorio's precociously Baroque Villa d'Este near Tivoli created for the wealthy Cardinal Ippolito d'Este of Ferrara in the latter half of that century.

The importance of Bramante's design of the Belvedere courtyard and gardens for Pope Julius II can hardly be exaggerated. With rising terraces joined by spectacular ramps and staircases, and spacious loggias and capacious niches ensconcing some of the most valuable statues of antiquity, it was a plan that would influence garden design for centuries.

Pirro Ligorio, too, was full of ideas. All Italian gardens from classical times had been cooled by fresh water in ponds and fountains, some of which attained a high level of beauty and complexity. But it is doubtful whether in any garden there was ever assembled such a varied and lovely combination of water, statuary and vegetation as in the Villa d'Este. Most notable is the row of a hundred fountains with water spurting from a hundred spouts into two long channels. Presiding over this refreshing scene is a large statue of the Sybil. Another feature of the gardens was the hydraulic mechanism which provided the music in the Grand Organ fountain. This may have produced harmonious sounds, but the Owl fountain presented the mechanical drama of a screeching owl scattering a bevy of songbirds by its sudden appearance in the middle of their concert. Though now much restored after a long period of decay, the Villa d'Este is unlikely to recover its pristine glory. Nevertheless it remains a supreme example of an Italian High Renaissance garden.

At about the same time as the Villa d'Este was being built by Pirro Ligorio after 1550, another architect was busy preparing plans for the pavilion and laying out the gardens of another villa at Bagnaia near Viterbo. It is almost certain that it was Jacopo Barozzi, called Il Vignola from his birthplace near Modena, who received the commission from the Bishop of Viterbo, Cardinal Francesco Gambara, to create the complex. This was to include a summer pavilion already erected, and now called the Villa Lante after the family

RIGHT: *Statuary in the garden of the Borromean palace on Isola Bella in Lake Maggiore, where there are superb views of the surrounding mountain scenery.*

FAR RIGHT: *The Amphitheatre at the southern end of Isola Bella is the most prominent feature of the garden with statues, rocaille decoration, niches, grottoes and obelisks, all surmounted by a rearing unicorn, the emblem of the Borromeo family.*

LEFT: *The fountain of Aeolus, god of the winds, in the garden of the Palace of Caserta in Campania north of Naples, which contains a lengthy water staircase interspersed with fountains and statuary.*

LEFT: *The Renaissance building of the Villa La Pietra near Florence, seen from the garden which was created in this century by an English owner, Arthur Acton, in a Florentine Renaissance style.*

RIGHT: *A balustrade of the terrace at La Pietra overlooking the lower parterre. The statues are eighteenth-century Venetian.*

RIGHT: *A fountain in the lower parterre at La Pietra surrounded by the typical low box hedges of the Renaissance garden, arranged symmetrically with garden walks and flower beds.*

which acquired it in 1656. This garden has been acclaimed as the most perfect and best preserved of the Renaissance gardens in Italy.

The Villa Lante does indeed appear to fulfill all the criteria for garden building laid down by the ancients – the hillside site overlooking a city, with familiar hills and mountains in the distance and in the foreground a delicacy of garden herbs and box hedges cut in geometrical designs, and fountains everywhere. The mingling of water with statuary and topiary in a series of fountains, pools and cascades which follow the axial line from the garden entrance to the central space between the pavilions is brilliantly developed – the most lovely expression of the physical beauty of nature in all Italy or in all the world was how Sacheverell Sitwell described it.

To examine the transition from the High Renaissance to the Baroque we shall not go south as you might expect but to the northern lake of Maggiore. There the Isola Bella (the 'beautiful island') in the western arm of the lake, once a bare rock, was transformed by various heads of the Borromeo family into what has been described as a masterpiece of Baroque extravaganza. A series of terraces was built up with rock and soil carried over from the mainland. In 1630, through the initiative of Count Carlo Borromeo in honour of his wife Isabella (after whom, with a small change, the island was named), the conversion of the bare rock began. After his death the continuing dedication of his sons and the skill of ingenious architects (among whom Angelo Crivelli of Milan was the chief planner of the garden and the buildings) and a host of sculptors, masons, painters and labourers, the rock was transformed into an incomparable pleasure garden with a palace at the north end of it. Although the plant life in the garden is nowadays rich and varied, it is the sculpture around the ponds and on the terraces which predominates.

We can conclude our look at Italian Baroque

gardens by considering that which adorns the Palace of Caserta near Naples. This has been described as the swansong of the Italian Baroque, though the palace itself may well be regarded as a herald of the new Neoclassical style. In 1751 the then King Charles III of Naples, a son of Philip V of Spain and of Elisabeth Farnese, commissioned Luigi Vanvitelli, the architect son of a well-known Dutch painter, to draw up plans for the palace and garden of Caserta. The palace is 3 kilometres (2 miles) from hills to the north, where the old medieval town of Caserta Vecchia is situated. The gardens extend the whole way to the Grand Cascade, a water-staircase set into the hills, which forms the apex of the view from the palace. The

ABOVE: *A view of the garden and stream from a balcony of the Villa Caetani at Ninfa, south of Rome. The water is transparent and the river-bed bright green with gently undulating sedge.*

LEFT: *The stream that flows through the whole length of the property at Ninfa is fed from a small lake replenished by springs in the mountain behind.*

LEFT: *The garden of the Palazzo Orsini at Bomarzo near Viterbo is situated on a hillside where outcrops of rock have been carved to resemble monsters or figures from antiquity, such as Ceres, the goddess of wheat, shown here.*

RIGHT: *The carved rock face of Orcus, the god of the underworld, at Bomarzo.*

centre-line of the gardens is formed by the shallow watercourses, leading from the palace to the Grand Cascade, intercepted every now and then by a waterfall and fountains pouring into a pond surrounded by Baroque statuary.

It was undoubtedly the manifold beauty of Italian gardens which was one of the major attractions drawing foreigners to Italy as visitors or residents. Among the many foreigners who came to stay a few turned out to be or became expert gardeners. It is worth looking at least at three of the gardens they created, which are among the finest in the country.

The first of these is the garden of the Hanbury villa at La Mortola on the Mediterranean coast just short of the French frontier. The 40-hectare (100-acre) property was bought in 1867 by Sir Thomas Hanbury, a wealthy China merchant, for his retirement. It extends from the coast road on the hillside downwards to the sea across the railway line at the bottom (and the track of what was once the Via Aurelia) to include a quite prominent headland. It is perhaps the only large tract of land on the riviera which is still entirely unspoilt by incongruous buildings and it gives one

a pang of regret to imagine what this marvellous coastline must have been like before falling prey to the developers.

At the time of the laying out and planning of the garden at La Mortola, Sir Thomas Hanbury was assisted by his brother Daniel, a botanist. In the course of time the garden became enriched with a greater variety of plants than any other garden in Italy. They were taken from every continent and from Japan. The mild climate and southern exposure on the open hillside ensured rapid growth. Only a few plants, including coffee, tea and sugar cane, failed to prosper. A lasting influence on the design of the garden was a young German horticulturalist, Ludwig Winter, who had been sacked by the Empress Eugenie for singing the Marseillaise in the Tuileries Gardens. He was the head gardener of La Mortola for seven years.

The Hanbury garden was more notable for its entrancing situation and the unique variety of its plants than for its design. When Sir Thomas died in 1907 after his brother Daniel, the estate was managed by Lady Hanbury. It was neglected during the First World War but revived somewhat between the wars during the stewardship of

Thomas Hanbury's daughter-in-law Dorothy, who in 1960 made over the estate to the Italian nation. After a period of neglect the management was taken over by the Botanical Faculty of the University of Genoa. Now under the dynamic control of Professor Paola Profumo, it shows signs of recovering its former stature.

An interesting example of a classical garden created by an Englishman in Italy is that of La Pietra near Florence. Here the villa was a fifteenth-century building renewed by Cardinal Capponi in 1650 and bought by Arthur Acton, a cultivated English art dealer with a rich American wife, in 1902. It was Acton's intention with the help of a Polish gardener to create a Tuscan garden at La Pietra. Although some of its features, like the widespread use of topiary, were undoubtedly derived from the Florentine Renaissance, the accommodation along the terraces of Acton's large collection of eighteenth-century Venetian statues and the arrangement of wisteria round a peristyle of roses on a pergola showed an individual taste with a strong English inclination for flowers. Thus La Pietra is a unique combination of devotion to the classical ideal of a garden and English delight in floral decoration.

The last of the gardens in whose creation foreigners were considerably involved is both unique and unforgettably beautiful. The name of no great architect is attached to its creation. No historic event attended its inception. It is true that it evolved under the aegis of one of the greatest and most cultivated of the ancient Roman families, the Caetani, but like so many things Italian its birth was due to a combination of unforeseeable circumstances.

The first of these was when the small medieval town of Ninfa, on the edge of the Pontine marshes, was overwhelmed in 1382 by its hostile neighbours from the nearby mountain communities and destroyed. It never recovered, perhaps because soon afterwards the marshes became infested with malaria. So Ninfa became a ruined town, with its buildings (except for the town hall), its lookout tower and its walls covered with ivy and with wild flowers growing in the streets.

The beginning of Ninfa's resurrection occurred when, after World War I, the owner Prince Gelasio Caetani, a brilliant engineer who had practised as a mining engineer in America, decided to restore the town hall as a country villa. He planted trees, among others the very Italian avenue of cypresses, in and around the estate, while his English mother planted the climbing roses which now cascade from the treetops and over many of the walls of the ancient city. After the death of Prince Gelasio the estate devolved on his brother Roffredo and his American wife Marguerite. Under her management the garden at Ninfa began to acquire its present look, with many flowering trees and shrubs, the construction of new paths and water-channels across the garden area, and the setting out of flowerbeds and borders. When her son Prince Camillo died during World War II, Ninfa was inherited by his sister Lelia Caetani. In 1951 she married Hubert Howard whose mother was a member of the Roman Giustiniani-Bandini family.

While Hubert managed the estate, Lelia beautified the garden; both showed an unusual capacity for conservation and innovation in their management and embellishment of the estate. Being childless they set up a trust which now controls the property and strives to maintain the high standards set by the Howards.

One more garden calls for attention: it is, like Ninfa, unique but nearer to Italian traditions perhaps than the romanticism of Ninfa. This is a garden of 'monsters', not, I am convinced, made to frighten so much as to amuse. At Bomarzo, 20 kilometres (12 miles) east of Viterbo, there is a castle on the hilltop above the town which belonged to the Orsini family. It was converted into a palazzo or villa (*c*.1552), which according to the custom of the time should have a garden attached to it. The summit on which the palace was perched offered no obvious place for laying out a garden in the traditional manner, and the owner, Pierfrancesco Orsini, who liked to be called Vicino and who must have been an eccentric, decided to site his garden in the valley below. Ignoring all the rules of Renaissance garden design, he planted a wood in an area of rocky outcrops, which were sculpted to represent an assortment of mythological beings, human and animal. The design of these strange creatures is attributed to Pirro Ligorio. Here, among many

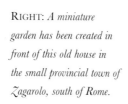

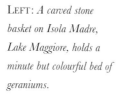

LEFT: *A carved stone basket on Isola Madre, Lake Maggiore, holds a minute but colourful bed of geraniums.*

RIGHT: *A miniature garden has been created in front of this old house in the small provincial town of Zagarolo, south of Rome.*

stone figures and animals, you will see Hercules tearing asunder the brigand Cacus; the local Venus of the Cimini hills; Father Tiber; the gaping mouth of the sea-god Glaucus, balancing a globe on his head, and that of Orcus the god of the underworld; and Ceres the corn goddess, crowned with a bread basket.

If it is extremely difficult to give more than a partial idea of the wealth and diversity, the beauty

A roof garden above the Spanish Steps in Rome.

and ingenuity of the large gardens in Italy, it is impossible to suggest the infinite variety of small private gardens which grace the innumerable terraces and courts of private houses. Nearly every palazzo in Rome and other cities has one or more terraces and nearly each terrace is a small garden. Here the soil must be hoarded in large terracotta

pots and vases, where fruit, mostly oranges and lemons, and bright flowers – geraniums, hisbiscus and salvia, for instance – are grown. Where a trellis or a pergola can be fixed, you will see wisteria, bougainvillea and honeysuckle providing colour and fragrance. The best way of having an informal meal in Italy is in an airy and secluded place with good food, the warmth of a summer evening, the perfume of the flowers, and friends.

DETAILS

ABOVE: *A drinking fountain in the Piazza del Mercato, Spoleto, Umbria.*

LEFT: *The courtyard of Fénis Castle in Aosta valley, Piedmont, is decorated with frescoes (c.1426) by Jaquerio.*

DOORS AND WINDOWS

*I*n the early classical period of Italian history, though monumental or religious buildings were surrounded by open colonnades, a dwelling house showed a blank and forbidding exterior. The exterior walls of a house were primarily protective; any openings in them were as small and inconspicuous as possible. Light was admitted to a building from an inner courtyard, and if a window appeared in an outside wall of a house, perhaps for the purpose of surveying the activities in the street, it would never be placed on the ground floor but high up in the second storey out of reach of any passers-by. Sometimes the main entrances were positioned at the top of a landing which was approached by an outside stairway. But if they were placed for convenience on the ground level, they would tend to be inconspicuous. This was also the case in the country. Farms were like small fortified castles.

In the late Roman Republic, and during the period of the Empire, more settled conditions made it possible for more building to be undertaken and for houses to open up. Wealthy Romans in particular, from the early Empire onwards, began to utilise the main front of their palaces and mansions as an advertisement for their wealth and good taste, a conceit which they inherited from the Etruscans. This gave great importance to the façade of a building and led to the construction of impressive portals and elegantly decorative windows of a size suitable to the grandness of the dwelling. This is observable in the remaining buildings of Pompeii and Herculaneum, like the House of Menandes in the former and the House of the Wooden Partition in

ABOVE: *The main entrance of the church of Santa Maria delle Grazie in Lecce, Apulia, designed by Michele Coluccio, a priest of the Theatine order (c.1590).*

ABOVE: *The elegant sixteenth-century doorway of the church of Santa Maria delle Cacce in Pavia, Lombardy, with clear-cut lines and contrasting colours.*

ABOVE: *Portal of the fifteenth-century Chiesa di Villa, in Castiglione Olona, Lombardy, is flanked by large statues of St Anthony (left) and St Christopher (right).*

ABOVE: *The doorway to the twelfth- or thirteenth-century church of Santa Maria Maggiore in Spello, Umbria, was refashioned in 1644, using a Romanesque frieze.*

the latter. And for decorative opulence we cannot fail to be impressed by descriptions of Nero's Domus Aurea or by the ruins of Hadrian's Villa at Tivoli.

The end of the Roman Empire (AD 476) was followed by a recession in building activity in the sixth and seventh centuries, and where new housing was erected in the countryside, it had perforce to present a fortified appearance. This security aspect of architecture, which placed a heavy restraint on the promotion of the decorative features of buildings, began to change as the Middle Ages advanced towards the fifteenth century. When the Florentine Renaissance emerged in the fifteenth century with the construction of Medicean villas in the countryside around the city and the first classical palazzi in its

ABOVE: *Door panels in the Via Gregoriana, Rome, near the Spanish Steps.*

streets, the doors and windows of these remarkable buildings were a strong element in their decoration.

The development of the Renaissance and Baroque styles, with a period of Mannerist intrusion between, can be observed in the construction of new palaces in Rome in the sixteenth century and in the great papal villas of the Counter-Reformation or the early seventeenth-century reconstruction of some of the villas at Frascati near Rome. These display the progressive enrichment of the door and window decoration of those periods. However, the decorative element does not always coincide with the period of the building to which it is applied. In any particular site the architect or decorator would follow models from any period which he

ABOVE: *Doorway to the house of the painter Federico Zuccari (1543-1609) in the Via Gregoriana, Rome.*

ABOVE: *The south door of the sixteenth-century Palazzo Orsetti, Lucca, with richly carved pilasters and arch.*

ABOVE: *Entrance to the eighteenth-century Baroque Palazzo Maggi in Martina Franca, Apulia.*

LEFT: *The heavily rusticated outline of this ancient doorway in Città di Castello, Umbria, is lightened by the use of wrought-iron work in the arch.*

LEFT: *A main portal of the Palazzo Motolese (1775), one of the principal Baroque palaces of Martina Franca, Apulia.*

LEFT: *The early Venetian-Gothic doorway of the Casa delle Aste near Strada Nuova in Venice.*

OPPOSITE: *A picturesque doorway in the small country town of Zagovrolo south of Rome.*

liked to use, or the decoration may have been added centuries after the building was completed. Nevertheless such a combination in the same building would be handled with taste and discretion and does not usually arouse a sense of discrepancy.

As we follow the development of architectural styles from the Roman period we can observe the gradual expansion of thematic material in stonework decoration. The earlier work in classical times, though employing some plants, was generally based on geometrical design and sculpted figures on tombs and monuments. The accompanying examples of doors and windows show how this ornamentation developed with decorative motifs of the classical period like rosettes, palmette leaves, lyres and vases of different shapes, as used by the Greeks, followed by festoons of cables and garlands of vines, or heads and human figures and the war panoply employed by the Romans. Moreover it was in Rome that a new type of frame for a wall opening appeared when the architects of the Roman Pantheon attached their aedicules (niches or small tabernacles) to the massive piers which support the dome. These aedicules served as models in countless Renaissance buildings and eventually even stirred echoes in the Reform Club of Pall Mall.

The Middle Ages contributed another set of decorative motifs to the embellishment of doors and windows, including biblical scenes like Trees of Jesse, the escutcheons of noble families, mythical monsters and the scroll-like foliage known as *rinceaux*, which enclosed strange human and animal figures.

Renaissance art made use of many existing motifs, adding some refinements but mostly improving, and increasing, the diversity of existing patterns in newly erected buildings. Thus, for instance, the decorative frieze around whole rooms or around doors became familiar features

ABOVE: *Façade of a late fourteenth- or early fifteenth-century palazzo in the Campo Sant' Angelo, Venice, with an assortment of ogee- and trefoil-arched windows.*

RIGHT: *Windows of the Palazzo Chigi in the Piazza Colonna, Rome, begun by Giacomo della Porta in 1562.*

BELOW: *Gothic arches and balcony of a late thirteenth- or fourteenth-century palazzo in the Corte Seconda del Milion, Venice.*

LEFT: *In the same house in Rome as the gaping mouth doorway illustrated on p.151 is this window to match. Such expressive themes were characteristic of the Mannerist style.*

LEFT: *The small Piazzetta Falconieri in Lecce, Apulia, enclosed by palazzi with elegant windows and balconies like this, provides fine examples of Lecce's eighteenth-century Baroque architecture.*

of decoration in the Renaissance and Baroque periods. Broken pedimental arches became common currency in the Mannerist epoch whether painted over doorways by decorators or used as solid stone capping for windows by architects. In the latter half of the sixteenth century Federico Zuccari in his Roman dwelling presented another contour for external doors and windows in the guise of a wide-open mouth. Earlier examples of this flight of fancy were to be seen in a large fireplace in the Palazzo Thiene at Vicenza and in the rocky entrance of a grotto in the Sacred Grove of the wood at Bomarzo, both of the early 1550s.

During the last century, and in this, a variety of styles might be associated in the same building, usually because craftsmen, like stucco artists or painter-decorators, carried out their work in a later epoch than that of the architectural design, but sometimes because of the reconstruction of part of an old building, as in the case of the façade of the old convent of San Silvestro in Rome (now the post office), where the architect chose the models of his windows on different floors from different periods. But the exercise of such eclecticism is not to be condemned out of hand, for it is undeniable, as our photographs amply demonstrate, that Italian architects and craftsmen, when fashioning the doors and windows of buildings in different regions of Italy during different periods, almost invariably maintained a very high standard of skill and inventiveness in their work.

LEFT: *Baroque-style windows with emphatically moulded arches and tympanum applied to a bank in the Corso Cavour, Città di Castello, Umbria.*

LEFT: *Windows in the first floor of seaside houses in Monterosso, Cinque Terre, Liguria, with* trompe l'oeil *classical-style frames.*

BELOW: *Decorative classical-style frame of the window of a modern house in Ischia Ponte, Campania.*

ABOVE: *Eighteenth-century windows and balconies on a house in Via Virgilio, Martina Franca, Apulia.*

LEFT: *The windows of the main post office in the Piazza San Silvestro, Rome, which was renewed in the nineteenth century by the Roman architect A. Malvezzi, exhibit a variety of revivalist styles.*

FRESCOES

The greatest period of Italian painting, which was also marked by the apotheosis of Italian wall paintings, began, if we can rely on a story told by Giorgio Vasari in his often accurate biography of Italian artists, around the year 1276. It was a time when the creativity of the Middle Ages, for long a period of rich artistic invention, was going into decline, and the Renaissance had not yet begun. It was then, according to Vasari's account, that the painter Cimabue (1240–1302), a member of a prosperous Florentine family, while making his way from Florence to nearby Vespignano, saw near the track along which he rode the recumbent figure of a shepherd guarding

RIGHT: *Herod's Banquet from the life of John the Baptist (1435), a fresco by the Florentine Masolino da Panicale in the baptistery adjoining the church of the Colleggiata in Castiglione Olona, Lombardy.*

BELOW: *Fresco of the Nativity in the eighth-century Tempietto ('little temple') Longobardo in Cividale del Friuli, Veneto.*

ABOVE: *An upper gallery in Fénis Castle in the Valle d'Aosta, Piedmont, with a fresco (c.1426) by Jaquerio showing philosophers and sages.*

his flock and wiling away the time by drawing with a stone stylus on a piece of slate the lifelike image of one of his sheep. Cimabue stopped to look and was so impressed by the youngster's talent that he asked the boy to become his pupil. Young Giotto replied that he would indeed like to do so if his father consented. Cimabue, who was already famous as a painter, made the required approach to Giotto's father, Bondone. He readily consented and soon afterwards the boy became a member of the Cimabue household. There his precocious talent soon outstripped even the skill of his master.

ABOVE: *The Adoration of the Shepherds (c.1501) by Pinturicchio in the Baglioni chapel of Santa Maria Maggiore, Spello, in Umbria.*

Giotto inaugurated a new era in Italian painting more markedly perhaps than any of his predecessors or successors. He made a complete break with the hieratic styles of Byzantine painting which for years had dominated Italian art. He introduced a new naturalism in his pictures which had such a wide appeal that it prepared the way for a return of classical realism when this was renewed in the Renaissance. His skill was widely employed in Florence, Assisi and Padua, where in the Capella degli Scrovegni (1303–5) is preserved his greatest masterpiece, a series of frescoes giving

the history of Redemption in thirty-eight scenes from the life of Jesus Christ and Mary, arranged in chronological order. The colour and narrative feeling were unlike anything seen before.

Fresco painting was probably known to the Greeks and was certainly used in the houses of Pompeii. A more developed technique of fresco painting was described in some detail by the Tuscan painter and writer Cennino Cennini (1370–1440) in his handbook for artists *Libro dell'Arte*. The painter must first prepare his surface by applying a thin, rough layer of plaster to be

covered with a second layer of much finer plaster. On the first layer the artist would sketch out a grid pattern of the distribution of the figures and masses in his painting. He would then draw an outline of the painting in broad brush strokes of a red wash. Once the outline of the painting was described on the ground coat of plaster, a final thin coat of wet plaster was laid over it day by day in sections. The painting of each section would then be completed while the top layer of plaster was still wet.

Vasari regarded fresco painting as the most skilful and beautiful method of applying colour to a wall. It demanded great experience from the artist and the ability to visualise his complete painting at each stage of its execution. He also had to be able to paint fast and to anticipate the changes which the paint would undergo when dry. Italian artists especially responded to the challenge and, except in Venice, where the damp atmosphere was unfavourable to the technique, fresco painting was practised by most of the

LEFT: *Detail of the ceiling of the Sala dei Giganti in Palazzo Doria Pamphili, Genoa. The fresco by Pierino del Vaga shows Jove hurling thunderbolts at the Giants (1529-33).*

RIGHT: *Part of another fresco by Pierino del Vaga in the Doria palace, Genoa. This depicts a popular historical theme about 'Carità Romana', a young Roman matron who succours a parched Roman soldier with her milk.*

greatest Italian artists. Indeed, if the great cycles of fresco painting in Italy were assembled into a single gallery, they would probably represent the finest collection of murals ever produced. Apart from Giotto's cycle in the Scrovegni chapel in Padua already mentioned, they would include Raphael's Stanze in the Vatican (1508–14); Michelangelo's ceiling of the Sistine Chapel with his vision of the Creation of Adam (1508); and works by Luca Signorelli, Pinturicchio, Masaccio, Masolino da Panicale and Piero della Francesca, to name but a few.

Such frescoes, produced during the two centuries when the art of the fresco reached its highest expression, were to set a standard of inventiveness, emotional intensity and beauty of conception and colour which was never repeated. Yet, from the accompanying illustrations it is clear that from the early days, well before the great period until long after its close, the skill of Italian artists in this peculiarly Italian mode of painting remained very high. The examples shown here come from many areas of the country, not only the most productive like Tuscany, Umbria and in or around Rome. We begin in the early Middle Ages in the remote and beautiful city of Cividale del Friuli, on the north-eastern frontier of Italy, with some frescoes of perhaps the ninth century and we end some thousand years later in one of the palaces of an ancient Roman city, Ascoli Piceno, now turned to good use as a social club, with its ancient salons refurbished with frescoes in the Neoclassical mode.

Along the way we shall see murals by the early fifteenth-century Gothic painter Giacomo Jaquerio, who, though not well known abroad, had a profound influence on the course of painting in Piedmont, Savoy and Switzerland. Some of his most important work is to be seen in the striking pictures of saints and prophets at the Abbazia di Sant' Antonio at Ranverso about 8 kilometres (5 miles) west of Turin. These he was to

ABOVE: *Fresco attributed to the school of Vasari in the Sala del Trono of the sixteenth-century Palazzo Vitelli in Città di Castello, Umbria.*

LEFT: *Detail of the graffito decoration by Giorgio Vasari (1512-74) on the garden façade of the Palazzo Vitelli, Città di Castello.*

reproduce in part with the aid of assistants in the chapel and courtyard of the castle of Fénis (1420–30) in the Valle d'Aosta.

Also in the north of Italy is Castiglione Olona, described as an oasis of Tuscany in Lombardy. The delightful small city which lies just north of Milan was the seat of the prominent Castiglione family. Its most famous member, a papal legate who became Bishop of Piacenza and later a cardinal, was Branda da Castiglione (1350–1443), who rebuilt his home town in the Tuscan image which he found so attractive. And to add to its renown he engaged one of the most famous painters of the day, the Florentine Masolino da Panicale, to decorate the baptistery of the collegiate church with scenes from the life of St John the Baptist (1435), one of which, portraying Herod's Banquet, is reproduced here. These frescoes are considered to be some of

the painter's best work.

The Baglioni family chapel in the church of Santa Maria Maggiore at Spello, a lovely Umbrian hill-town, contains works by one of the fresco painters referred to above, Pinturicchio. Executed in 1501, these are the three great wall paintings of the Annunciation, the Adoration of the Shepherds (illustrated here) and the Disputation in the Temple, which show his brilliant handling of light and colour.

For a vivacious display of Mannerist panache we must go to Andrea Doria's palace at Fassolo in Genoa. Here the great Ligurian admiral and statesman was preparing his residence as a suitably sumptuous abode for his patron, the Emperor Charles V, on his visits to Genoa in 1529 and 1533. For this task he was able in 1529 to obtain the services of one of Raphael's most gifted assistants in Rome, who had fled the city before the impending sack by the emperor's army in 1527. This painter was Pierino del Vaga, who between 1529 and 1533 painted an assembly of ancestral Doria heroes in Medicean costume in the Loggia degli Eroi. In other rooms he displayed famous legends like the Carità Romana, and in the Sala dei Giganti a vigorous portrayal of the Gigantomachy, the war of the gods against the giants, where Jove is seen hurling his thunderbolts against the already prostrate giants.

Città di Castello is another small Umbrian city filled with art treasures, including the garden façade of the Palazzo Vitelli alla Cannoniera, where Vasari used graffito decoration to cover the wall surface with intricate patterns in grey and white. The technique of graffito first produced on wall paintings in the Middle Ages consists of applying two layers of differently coloured plaster to the wall and securing a pictorial or decorative effect by scratching a design through the darker top layer to contrast with the lighter underlayer. Some of the rooms of the palace are also heavily

frescoed. Those in the main Salone were painted by Cola dell'Amatrice in 1537. He was a well-known architect and painter in central Italy in the first half of the sixteenth century.

In the seventeenth, eighteenth and early nineteenth centuries a large amount of wall painting, some of excellent quality, was executed by painters of more limited renown than those dealt with so far. In the seventeenth century Ulisse Giocchi of Monte San Savino painted scenes from the life of St Agnes Segni in the convent which she had founded in Montepulciano near Siena. The Roman Ciro Ferri was one of the decorators of Villa Falconieri near Rome, where his frescoes of Proserpina and of the Allegory of Spring, considered his masterworks, were painted in the latter half of the seventeenth century. He was a collaborator of the famous Pietro da Cortona, with whom he had worked in the Palazzo Pitti in Florence. Stefano Tofanelli from Lucca was for a while prominent in Rome and then became the official painter at the court of Napoleon's sister Elisa Baciocchi, when she ruled in Lucca at the beginning of the nineteenth century. Not very long before that he was decorating the walls of the Villa Mansi near Lucca. And finally the main salons of the sixteenth-century Palazzo Sgariglia Dalmonte (now a club) in Ascoli Piceno were very agreeably frescoed in the Neoclassical style with pattern and figure decoration by the local artist Raffaele Fogliardi during the early years of the last century.

It would not be fitting to close this chapter without mention of that latecomer to the art of Italian fresco painting, Tiepolo (1696–1770), who turned out to be as remarkable as the great exponents of the fifteenth and sixteenth centuries. Whether in the archbishops' palaces in Udine or in Würzburg, at the Villa Valmarana in Vicenza, the Palazzo Labia in Venice or the Royal Palace in Madrid, the richness of his invention, the beauty of his colour schemes and the vivacity of his human subjects were without rival.

TOP: *Detail of an early nineteenth-century Neoclassical fresco by Raffaele Fogliardi in one of the main salons of the Palazzo Sgariglia Dalmonte, Ascoli Piceno, Marche.*

ABOVE: *Section of a fresco in early nineteenth-century Neoclassical style on a bedroom wall in the Villa Mansi, Segromigno, Tuscany.*

ABOVE: *La Primavera ('Spring'), a fresco in the sixteenth-century Villa Falconieri in Frascati, near Rome, painted by the Roman Ciro Ferri in the seventeenth century.*

FOUNTAINS

*T*he Roman love of water was apparent in constant manifestations of its use for the purposes not only of survival but also of refreshment and ornament. It became one of the means by which a ruler might ingratiate himself most successfully with the people. This was achieved by the provision of an ample water supply not only directly to the houses of the wealthy but by a network of hydrants all over Rome for public washing, drinking and cooking.

ABOVE: *Designed by Giacomo della Porta in the sixteenth century, the Fontana del Moro in Piazza Navona, contains the statue of a moor and a dolphin by Bernini.*

LEFT: *The Fontana delle Tartaruge (1581-4) in the Piazza Mattei, Rome, also designed by della Porta, features four youths holding tortoises by Taddeo Landini of Florence.*

RIGHT: *The Fontana dei Fiumi (1648-51), or Fountain of the Four Rivers, in the centre of the Piazza Navona, Rome, has four large figures representing the Rivers Danube, Nile, Plate and Ganges.*

Large quantities of water were also needed for the great public baths. Diocletian's baths (AD 302) could accommodate 3,000 bathers at any one time, while during Constantine's reign a decade later 1,352 hydrants were in action in Rome.

To supply the enormous amount of water to meet these requirements, which went far beyond the capacity of local springs and wells, the Romans constructed aqueducts displaying remarkable building and engineering skills.

In his two-volume account of Rome's water

supply the great Roman expert on aqueducts, Sextus Julius Frontinus, gave the amount of water brought in by the aqueducts at the end of the first century as more than 218 million gallons each day. The barbarian invasions of the fifth century destroyed the functioning of the aqueducts and very little was done to repair them until the advent of Pope Hadrian I (772–95), who during a period of peace procured by his Frankish protectors was able to carry out the repair of many churches and the reconstruction of four of the main aqueducts, but for the most part the inhabitants, now greatly reduced in number, had recourse to the river or to the wells for their water.

The great era of papal fountain building was well under way before the Renaissance period had started in Rome, with the restoration of several main aqueducts from earlier times. In 1447 the great Florentine humanist and architect Leon Battista Alberti restored the Virgo aqueduct for Pope Nicholas V, and this was once again repaired under Sixtus IV (1471–84), a great and spendthrift builder. In 1492 Pope Innocent VIII channelled a number of springs on the Vatican hill and the water of the decrepit aqueduct of Trajan into an old fountain in St Peter's Square. However, it was not until the next century, the memorable Cinquecento, that Romans began to see fountains of unimagined beauty appearing in many of the squares in their city.

Among the great number of well-known fountains in Rome we can select only a few for consideration here. The choice, however, will illustrate the great variety of these admirable ornaments, which through the centuries became one of the city's main attractions. The great age of the Roman fountains began with Pope Gregory XIII (1572–95) and his Roman-born but Lombard-bred architect Giacomo della Porta. One of his first commissions was for the fountain in Piazza Colonna at the very centre of Rome, which dates from 1575. It was fed by the Aqua

The Naiad fountain in the Piazza della Repubblica, Rome. The main basin was constructed in 1885, the naiads added in 1901 and the central figure in 1914.

Virgo and because that source was unable to supply much of a head of water the fountain is set very low. A small jet flows into an upper cup whose overflow drips into a large basin. Two more small jets protrude from the water of the basin to give a few ripples to the smooth surface. The effect of the whole is one of soothing simplicity. However, the effect is obtained not merely by the elementary forms employed but by a quite complex mixture of marbles, ranging from the Carrara vase at the top to the Porta Santa marble

in the lower basin and the travertine base.

Much smaller than the Colonna fountain but considered by some authorities the most beautiful of all the fountains of Rome is that which graces the diminutive Piazza Mattei. It is known as the Fontana delle Tartarughe ('tortoises') and it was also designed by Giacomo della Porta. Here all the elements combine to perfection. The shallow upper bowl is of a veined Greek marble called *bigio morato* in Italy. It is supported by a sculpted stem of Serravazze marble from the Apuanian Alps and

ABOVE: *The Rococo Fontana di Trevi in the Via di San Vicenzo, Rome, was designed in 1732 by Nicolò Salvi (c.1751) and completed in 1762. The last of the great Roman fountains, it became the most popular of all.*

rests on a base of Carrara marble from the same region. The four large shells projecting over the lower basin are, however, carved from polychrome breccia from Teos in Asia Minor. Between these shells and the upper bowl four beautiful bronze youths maintain the balance of

their precarious posture, each helping a turtle over the rim into the upper bowl with one hand, while with the other holding the tail of a dolphin, on the head of which one foot is gracefully poised.

The sculptor of the four adolescents was the Florentine Taddeo Landini, a pupil of the much more famous Giambologna. Landini completed the fountain in 1585, all but the tortoises. These were added during a restoration of the fountain in 1658, and this was perhaps a stroke of genius by Bernini. They provide the final and most magical touch to what is a masterpiece of irresistible surprises. This fountain, according to one of the most expert writers on Rome, Georgina Masson, probably holds the palm, even among the fountains of Rome, for sheer delight. And what other country but Italy, she asks, could have produced it?

Another example of della Porta's fountain design is to be seen in the Piazza Campitelli, with Carlo Rainaldi's fine church of Santa Maria in Campitelli on one side and three sixteenth-century palaces, two of them attributed to della Porta, on the other. This is a traditional type of fountain with two basins. A central jet in the upper produces an overflow all round the rim into the much larger lower basin which is raised about a metre (just over 3 feet) above ground. The fountain was erected in 1589 and is built of marble.

Among the fountains designed in 1575 by della Porta, there was one at either end of Piazza Navona with a polygonal cup of Portadente marble above a larger basin of Carrara marble sunk into the ground. The one at the south end was embellished by statues of Tritons which were later removed to adorn the lake of the Villa

ABOVE: *A small Baroque fountain with a frescoed background decorates a niche in a palazzo courtyard in Rome.*

Borghese in 1874 and replaced by copies. This fountain was decorated in 1653 by the statue of a moor designed by Bernini and carved by G. A. Mari – a powerful, irate-looking figure struggling with a large, writhing fish. Also in Piazza Navona is the great central Fontana dei Fiumi (Fountain of the Four Rivers), an outstanding masterpiece which was designed by Bernini for Pope Innocent X and carved and assembled from 1648 to 1651. In addition to the four river-figures of the Danube, the Nile, the Plate and the Ganges (the latter with an oar), the fountain contained a palm tree, a lion and a horse. These items have been attributed to Bernini's own hand. When in 1651 the pope made a visit to the site before the inauguration of the fountain, Bernini excused himself because the pipes were not ready for the water to begin flowing. Then as the pope turned to go, the conduits were opened and Innocent looked back

in amazement as the fountain came alive.

With the ending of the seventeenth century the great age of papal fountain-building drew to a close. It is therefore somewhat astonishing that the most spectacular and the most famous of the Roman fountains, the Fontana di Trevi, was not completed until 1762 under Pope Clement XIII. The work was put in hand in 1732 by his predecessor Clement XII, under the direction of the Roman architect Nicolò Salvi, whose design was chosen from among those of other architects, although his only previous achievement of note was a construction for the launch of a firework fête in the Piazza di Spagna. He made the fountain his life's work. It was to be fed by the waters of the ancient Aqua Virgo, the channel for which was built by Agrippa from springs 13 kilometres (8 miles) outside Rome on the way to Tivoli. It was the purest of all the waters carried to Rome in aqueducts but its flow had been intermittent.

Salvi's creation was by no means entirely original, and the Baroque façade which was applied to the rear of the Palazzo Poli to form the background to the fountain, has none of the merit of a work by Michelangelo or even by Vanvitelli. It is when we reach the lower level of this ornate

ABOVE: *The Mascherone fountain (seventeenth to eighteenth century) in the Piazza Campello, Spoleto, Umbria.*

ABOVE: *Named after the donor, the Fontanella Sen (1571) in Asolo, Veneto, is still in constant use.*

ABOVE: *The Fontana dei Delfini, one of a series of magnificent eighteenth-century fountains set in 3 kilometres (2 miles) of watercourses in the park of the Royal Palace of Caserta, Campania.*

theatrical scenery that we may feel that Salvi has expressed a touch of genius. From the central niche of a triumphal arch in the Baroque façade, which dissolves at its base into a Rococo scramble of irregular rock and water lines, there emerges the commanding figure of Neptune standing on a huge conch-like chariot drawn forward by two winged sea-horses, which are led through the maze of boulders and waterfalls by Tritons. One of these blows into a seashell to animate his steed (known as the placid horse) while his companion throws up his arms to restrain the forward surge of the other stallion (known as the wild horse). The chariot is being drawn down a series of three oval basins into the large low-lying pool at the bottom

RIGHT: *The great fountain at the centre of the Piazza Pretoria in Palermo, Sicily, was imported from Florence in 1593, having been made about twenty years earlier.*

RIGHT: *The sixteenth-century Fontana della Natura in the gardens of the Villa d'Este, Tivoli, representing Mother Nature in the form of Diana of Ephesus.*

of the small piazza. Through this pool there pass about 80 million litres (17.5 million gallons) of water a day, some of which is carried on to feed the fountains in Piazza Farnese, Piazza Navona and Piazza di Spagna. In order to supply pressure for the spouts of the fountain, and height for the falls, the water is also gathered by pumps into a large tank behind the scenes.

The building of fountains has continued in Rome without interruption but only a few modern ones are noteworthy. Among those of the last century there was the very large round bowl set in one of the most spacious squares, the Piazza Esedra, now called the Piazza della Repubblica, in a part of the city covered by the ancient ruins of the baths of Diocletian and now also by modern buildings. With a rapidly rising population in the 1880s, Rome was expanding quickly. In the area near the station the Piazza Esedra was laid out,

half enclosed by a line of office and residential buildings which followed the curve of the exedra of the baths. In the centre of the piazza a circular fountain with a very high jet (1885) was the focal point. At the beginning of this century (1901) smaller circular basins around the central bowl were added, in which four bronze groups of naiads playing with sea monsters flaunt their voluptuous charms. In the centre a struggle portraying Victorious Man Triumphing over Brute Nature was later added (1914). All these sculptures were completed by the Sicilian Mario Rutelli of Palermo.

Thousands of other pleasing examples of fountains can be seen in towns and country houses all over Italy. Here we show a selection from the village of Asolo in the foothills of the Alps, from the town of Spoleto in Umbria and from the garden of the grandiose Palace of Caserta near Naples, already referred to in the previous chapter. One of the most complete and varied collection of fountains in the gardens of any villa is to be found at the Villa d'Este, described in the previous chapter.

The love of fountains was not confined to the mainland of Italy. In Sicily too there are lovely fountains, such as the sixteenth-century fountain of Piazza Pretoria in Palermo, made by Francesco Camilliani and Michelangelo Naccherino. Although Italy is not endowed with heavy rainfall and is in certain areas notoriously dry, the mountainous regions that cover a large part of the country form a huge reservoir of water, which in winter is frozen. In the spring and summer this reservoir is released in thousands of torrents. Down the centuries water has been stored, carried and plentifully used all over the country.

The spectacular jets of the Neptune fountain at the Villa d'Este, Tivoli, are situated between Pirro Ligorio's extraordinary Organ fountain and a long line of fishponds.

COLOURS

*N*o one will deny that Italy is a colourful country or that the Italians themselves have an eye for colour. Nature provides them with a rich and crowded palette: from sunsets on the mountain crests of the Dolomites to those on the waters of the Gulf of Taranto; from the delicate distant blue of Tuscan hills to the ultramarine of the Bay of Naples; from the green of the fresh shoots in the paddy fields of the Po Valley to that of the new corn in the Tavoliere of Apulia; from blossom-filled, snow-white almond orchards in Sicily to the banks of scarlet and purple bougainvillaea cascading over the terraced hillsides of the Ligurian coast.

The Italians' love of colour found expression in their art from the very beginning. In this as in nearly every aspect of their artistic development the Italians were inspired, and in the early stages guided, by the example of Greece. Perhaps the fact that very little of the work of the great Greek

ABOVE: *The comfortable and richly coloured furnishings of a Venetian gondola.*

ABOVE: *Brightly painted boats and houses in the Fondamenta Cavanella, Burano, an island near Venice.*

painters has survived, has deprived us of an understanding of how deeply Greek civilization was affected by colour. We greatly admire the remarkable Greek temples in Magna Graecia as we observe their grand outlines, their perfect proportions and meticulous masonry, but we have some difficulty visualising them adorned with bright colours as they first appeared to their votaries. The Romans in classical times, who admired every aspect of Greek art as reflecting the summit of civilization, will have imbibed a sense of colour in art from their familiarity with Greek buildings like the temples, where the painting of the external decoration was thick and bright as a peacock, and from the internal decoration of houses.

With an increasing number of skilled artists; with newly discovered techniques in the application of colour to surfaces; with more and

more surfaces becoming available through the growth of cities and within them of churches and palaces; with the rebirth of the classical Roman villa during the Renaissance, the opportunity of using colour to their heart's content became available to the Italians who were able to afford it in their homes and public buildings. We have dealt with some aspects of this blossoming upsurge of colour consciousness in the section about Frescoes (pp.156-61). It would be appropriate, however, to deal here with one aspect of colour in Italy, the use of colour washes on the exterior of buildings, a practice which is still widespread in certain regions of Italy, especially in the north.

Some of the examples shown here come from the coastal regions on opposite sides of Italy – the

Cinque Terre in Liguria, and Burano, one of the islands in the Venetian lagoon. The hamlet of Groppo lies on the steep mountain flank above a small seaside town called Manarola, one of the Cinque Terre, with cliffs falling to the sea in front of it and vineyards rising up behind it, out of which the red, yellow, pink and brown houses of Groppo emerge rather stridently. These are part of a new wave of housing which has been developed since the prolongation of the road linking the small towns along the coast north of La Spezia. The exterior decoration of houses along the Ligurian riviera with colour washes of varying intensity goes back to the fifteenth century and has

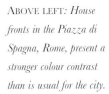

ABOVE: *A house in the Quartiere San Mauro provides another example of the vivid colouring on the island of Burano in the Venetian lagoon.*

ABOVE LEFT: *House fronts in the Piazza di Spagna, Rome, present a stronger colour contrast than is usual for the city.*

LEFT: *A striking yet harmonious range of colours is displayed by the houses of Groppo clinging to the hill above Manarola, one of the Cinque Terre in Liguria.*

LEFT AND CENTRE LEFT: *The cloister of the Franciscan convent of Santa Chiara in Naples was transformed in 1742 by the Neapolitan Domenico Vaccaro, who used majolica tiles depicting landscapes, rustic scenes, fruit, etc. to cover the pillars of the pergola and the bench seats.*

CENTRE RIGHT: *A small pillar, faced with majolica tiles, in the Piazza A. Diaz, Anacapri, on the island of Capri.*

LEFT: *Garden terrace of a third floor apartment in Naples. The parapet seat is strikingly decorated by nineteenth-century majolica tiles.*

produced such charming municipal kaleidoscopes as Sestri Levante, Portofino and Camogli.

At the other side of Italy in the Venetian lagoon, on the island of Burano, not only the houses but the boats moored alongside the canal banks are decked out in the brightest colours. Venetian houses, however, are mostly painted in milder colours than those of Burano, though some of the public transport, like a gondola with its crimson upholstery, is in a small way as colourful as a London bus. The city whose colours I have most relished, through my long acquaintance with it in all seasons, is Rome. The washes on the walls of brick or stone vary through shades of red and brown to burnt sienna, orange, yellow ochre, white and black and grey. The season and the time of day lay their veneer on each surface – the clarity of the morning light in winter, the midday haze, the glow of a summer evening. The Romans sometimes also like strong contrasts, as can be seen in the photograph of the houses at the end of Piazza di Spagna, where the bright cream strip of a narrow house front contrasts strikingly with the brilliant red façades of the eighteenth-century houses on either side.

The Interiors chapter (pp.70-133) displayed the colour and variety of Italian decoration. Nor was it only indoors that colours were lavishly employed. In the courtyard of a palace, the terrace of an urban apartment, the centre of a piazza or the cloister of a convent we may see, in addition to flowers, walls and pillars covered in bright majolica tiles. But the joy which Italians derive from bright colours is not confined to the owners of grand houses. It is shared by all the people. A great number of local pageants attest this craving, such as the famous medieval Palio di Siena – the most colourful horse-race in Europe – and the Historical Regatta in Venice, a race of gondolas and small boats on the Grand Canal, first contested in 1315. (An excellent portrayal can be seen in Canaletto's painting of it in the National

Gallery.) In the Gioco di Calcio, a Florentine ball game, the players are dressed in the original sixteenth-century costume, which was more chromatic than functional. The umpire, dressed like King Philip II of Spain, brandishes a sword to validate his controversial decisions. These are sporting events, but there is much pageantry too in religious processions on the principal feasts of the Church all over the country, and events of local historical importance are often re-enacted with great display.

Although not so generally addicted to gardening as the English, Italians like to demonstrate their love of colour with flowers. It is quite a common sight to see flowers tastefully arranged in window boxes. In some places a kind of flower show has grown up, it would seem spontaneously, to celebrate a feast or for some other purpose. One famous exhibition of this kind was held each year in the Umbrian hill-town of Spello for the Feast of Corpus Christi. Here, on a stretch over a kilometre in length leading up to the main church, flower blooms of every kind were assembled to form a veritable mosaic of different themes, some figurative (like a Pietà) others geometric (like the façade of a church). The freshly picked flowers provided a feast of colour enlivened by the fragrance of exquisite perfumes. Another such floral display was mounted in the small town of Genzano in the Alban hills south of Rome. In Rome itself, since the early 1960s, there has prevailed a most praiseworthy custom during the months of April and May of covering the entire three flights of the Spanish steps from top to bottom with rows of banked azaleas. The sight is unforgettable and provides as much delight for the Romans as it does for the tourists.

If Italian art and life are full of exuberance, as travellers so often find, a main ingredient in the preservation of this happy state of affairs is the colour which can be seen all over Italy.

STONEWORK

*M*uch of the splendour of Italian buildings, inside and out, depends on the quality of the materials with which they have been erected and adorned. Among these materials the most beautiful is stone, whether used for structural or decorative purposes. Italy is a country particularly well endowed with deposits of stone for carving or cladding, building and dressing. The accessibility of quarries in the neighbourhood of most of the main cities has led to the formation of numerous groups of skilled stoneworkers, who provided a succession of great sculptors and architects of renown in almost every generation.

Stone was available to builders and sculptors from all parts of Italy. We need only think of some

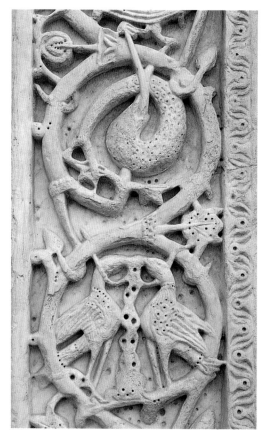

ABOVE: *Grotesque masks enliven a well-head in the cloister of San Martino, Naples.*

LEFT: *A detail of the portal in the north façade (1133-1201) of the cathedral of San Feliciano, Foligno, Umbria.*

LEFT: *Carrara marble quarries at Colonnata in the Apuanian Alps, Tuscany.*

of the great buildings in Italian cities to be assured of this. In Rome, for instance, the ancient theatre of Marcellus, whose remnants now form the foundations of the Palazzo Orsini, the Colosseum, the warmly embracing arms of the colonnade of St Peter's and large parts of the basilica itself remind us of the copious deposits of travertine stone beneath the Sabine hills in the Campagna of Rome. In Venice the limestone of Istria was constantly in use for the construction of the great palaces and the churches of the city – a dazzling white stone which was easy to carve but which weathered admirably and could be transported quickly across the gulf and into the lagoon in ships. Though more reliant on brick than stone,

Milan was able to draw excellent granite from quarries on the west side of Lake Maggiore and other stone from the neighbourhood of Lugano. The white stone of the Viuggiù quarries was widely used. Not much further away, in the opposite direction near Brescia, were the limestone quarries from which the white Botticino marble was extracted and employed in the construction of the glaringly grandiose monument to King Victor Emmanuel II near the Capitol in Rome. Florence had its quarries of Settignano, Maiano and Carmignano nearby. These yielded the smooth blue-grey *pietra serena*, used so effectively by Michelangelo in the New Sacristy of the church of San Lorenzo to delineate the framework of his famous Medicean tombs. Genoa was close to the quarries of its well-known dark Portoria stone, and Lavagna with its fine slate tiles was not far down the coast.

In the south of Italy, in Apulia, the intricate carvings on church and palace façades in the delightful city of Lecce were fashioned from the honey-gold sandstone called *pietra leccese*, of which many layers lie close to the surface of the fields and vineyards in the countryside. This is another stone which is soft when extracted and therefore easy to carve but which hardens when exposed to the air. Lecce was full of building activity in the seventeenth and eighteenth centuries when the best of the Lecce Baroque architecture was conceived. Another masterpiece of southern Baroque art was the Royal Palace at Caserta, north of Naples. This was built almost entirely of travertine from the Bellona quarries near Capua, and of tufa from the quarries of Santa Nicola la Strada just south of Caserta. In Sicily the exterior of the fine Palazzo Biscari in Catania exhibits an intriguing contrast of the white stone of Syracuse for the decoration with a dark plaster for the walls made from the crushed lava of Etna.

Of all the types of stone mentioned above, marble has been more generally prized than any other since the beginning of our era because of its beauty, flexibility and range of colour. Though

ABOVE: *Detail of the carved marble frame of the main door (c.1300) of Orvieto Cathedral, Umbria, showing prophets entwined in the branches of a Tree of Jesse.*

there are rich deposits of different kinds of marble in many different places in Italy, that which is extracted from the Apuanian mountains in Tuscany, at the foot of which lie the small towns of Massa and Carrara, is by far the most famous. The stone from this region was employed from the third century BC by the Romans, and the famous 'white marble' (*marmor lunense*) was incorporated in many of the monuments of ancient Rome, like Trajan's Column and the Pantheon. The pure white marble, owing to its tractability, was highly prized by the sculptors of the Renaissance. Michelangelo's exquisite Pietà in St Peter's is carved from a block of this type of marble.

The existence of readily accessible quarries is obviously not the whole, or even the main, explanation for the vast amount of outstanding stonework to be found in every corner of Italy.

The human factor, the artist and the patron, are clearly even more important. Greek architects and sculptors were widely employed in Rome during the Hellenistic period (*c*.323 to 29 BC). Wealthy Romans, who spoke Greek fluently and liked to travel in Greece – for this was the hallmark of a cultivated man – not only built their mansions and villas in and around Rome or Naples in the Greek style but filled them with Greek-inspired statuary, paintings, mouldings and mosaics. The artists who provided these attractions at that time must have been Greeks or Egyptians. Outstanding monuments of Roman antiquity, like the marble Ara Pacis (13 BC), were the work of Greek sculptors, while a

ABOVE: *Some of the remarkable carving in the abbey church of Vezzolano, near Turin, is shown in this section of the rood-screen (c. 1189).*

ABOVE: *A section of the carved pilaster framing the main entrance to the Palazzo Orsetti, Lucca.*

BELOW: *Part of the stone carving on a sixteenth-century drinking fountain at the front of the town hall in Spello, Umbria.*

ABOVE: *Renaissance detailing on the façade (by Mauro Codussi) of San Zaccaria, Venice.*

LEFT: *Well-head in the Piazza Grande, Montepulciano, Tuscany, with sculptures of griffins and two lions supporting the Medici coat of arms.*

Greek or Greco-Syrian architect, Appollodurus of Damascus, designed and supervised the construction (AD 113) of the marble column of Trajan in the Roman Forum with its remarkable spiralling frieze portraying the emperor's major battles against the Dacians and containing 2,500 sculptured figures.

It was not only from Greece itself that Italian patrons recruited their workforce of artists. For a thousand years before the beginning of the Roman Empire Greek traders and colonists had established themselves in southern Italy and Sicily, which came to be known as Magna Graecia. This region produced a number of city-states and a flourishing artistic and intellectual culture, which was not extinguished when from the fourth century BC onwards Roman power replaced Greek control in the southern part of the Italian peninsula. It is therefore reasonable to conclude that the artists who built and decorated the houses of the wealthy Roman aristocracy in Pompeii and Herculaneum, before the small towns were devastated by the eruption of Mount Vesuvius in AD 79, were for the most part Greek or of Greek origin. The works of art which emerged when the ruins were uncovered in the eighteenth and nineteenth centuries disclosed not only rich domestic architecture but astonishingly beautiful interior decoration – paintings, mosaics, carved mouldings and statuary. Here undoubtedly was a skilled workforce which would hand on their expertise to future generations born in Italy.

The native Italian artists were, however, reinforced by more foreigners who arrived in various waves. After Constantine's establishment of his capital in Constantinople a new artistic centre was created from which sculptors, architects and painters were to drift westwards into Italy where patronage remained strong. Another source of expert stone-carvers appeared, independently of Greek and Roman influence, in northern Italy around the lakes of Lugano and

Mannerist-style sculpture decorates the late fifteenth-century Casa Longobarda in Asolo, Veneto, built – it is thought – by Francesco Grazioli, an architect descended from the Lombard stonemasons who emigrated to the Veneto.

Como. These sculptors and architects are referred to as the Comacine masters. They were most active in the eleventh century, although they had already been mentioned in an edict of the Lombard King Rothari in the seventh, and they played a major part in the development of Romanesque art in Italy.

The Romanesque style enjoyed wide diffusion in most parts of Italy, and the requirement for sculptural decoration on the façades of the great churches brought forth a new generation of stonemasons and carvers, which proved to be the most productive in Italy until that time. The style was favoured by the Church as a means for propagating its teachings. In Apulia the outstandingly beautiful Romanesque cathedrals were mainly built during the period of Norman rule (1054–1194) after the expulsion of the previous Byzantine rulers of the region. The new Norman overlords probably brought some of their northern stone-carvers to supervise the decoration of the new cathedral churches, though many of the sculptors and mosaic artists who worked under Norman rule were undoubtedly of Byzantine origin. In Sicily, too, where the Romanesque achieved a remarkable development under the Normans, the style was adapted by Norman,

Byzantine and Saracen artists to create an amalgam of all their tastes.

The last years of Romanesque building in Italy coincided with the adoption in some places of a new style imported from France and now called Gothic. Some of the great Italian cathedrals like those of Siena (1245–80), Orvieto (1290–1600), Florence (1296–1421) and Milan (1385–1813) were mainly Gothic in design, while some of the important abbeys which were built by the Cistercian order, like the monastery of Fossanova (1187–1208) in the hills between Rome and Naples, followed the early Gothic Burgundian style. The churches of Santa Maria sopra Minerva in Rome and San Francesco in Assisi are Gothic, but in the south the style was rarely adopted.

Medieval cathedrals were the handiwork of closely knit communities of painters, glass workers, mosaicists, metal workers and sculptors; none, however, were as important as the sculptors, who were often architects as well. Of all the great Italian Gothic cathedrals the largest, and the last to be completed, was that of Milan. Built entirely of the rose white marble of Candoglia in Val d'Ossola, this late Gothic cathedral, inside and out, is embellished by an array of 3,159 statues, not to mention the 96 gigantic gargoyles serving as water-spouts. In addition to the churches the Italian Communes of the eleventh and twelfth centuries provided many examples in northern and central Italy of fine secular public buildings in the Gothic style – town halls and castles exhibiting much admirable stonework – but by far the greatest developments in stone-carving were those ushered in by the Renaissance.

From the fifteenth century onward the demand for stonework decoration increased enormously not only to meet the continuing and growing demands of the Church but also to satisfy the desire for ostentation of a rapidly expanding class of merchants and bankers in the many important cities of Italy. In the sixteenth and seventeenth centuries Italy contained some of the wealthiest states in Europe and her cities were among the largest and finest on the continent. The patronage of great civic families like the Medici and that of the popes was met by an alignment of artists of quite exceptional quality and versatility of talent. Their output was prodigious. Many artists were also gifted interior decorators and some were designers of stage sets at the courts of Italian princes.

The display of fine stone-carving was to be seen on the outside of buildings around portals and windows, on friezes and balconies, in pediments and arcades. External statuary found new

A crowd of sculpted figures form part of the Venus and Adonis fountain in the park of the Royal Palace of Caserta, Campania, designed by Luigi Vanvitelli in 1751.

footholds on the rooftops of Palladian villas, on ornamental balustrades and as the centrepieces of fountains. Although interior decoration in the way of furniture was slow to develop until the eighteenth century and stone furnishings were rare except in churches, a great deal of decoration was lavished, from the Renaissance onward, on walls and ceilings, especially in the reception rooms on the *piano nobile* of palaces and villas. In these grand salons stonework was used to frame doorways and chimneypieces; it was sometimes also used on friezes but was frequently found in the form of statues, such as busts of members of the family set on a mantel or carved console along the wall.

The classical repertoire of stone carving was enriched in Italy by stone cutters from France and Lombardy bringing new themes derived from hunting and chivalry and new shapes like large hooded fireplaces. The synthesis of classical and medieval forms, begun by the Pisano family, received a great impetus in the Renaissance with the rediscovery of classical art and the deeper understanding of its meaning achieved by the humanists. The revival of the nude human figure in the round, probably first achieved after 1430 by Donatello with his small bronze figure of David, who reappeared standing 5.5 metres (18 feet) tall in Michelangelo's vast marble statue of 1504, was the beginning of a great expansion in the scope of sculpture. The bustling cupids of classical Roman art re-emerged as the mischievous putti of the Renaissance and especially the Baroque. Between the carefully moulded proportion and perfection of Italian Renaissance forms and the relaxation and ostentation of the Baroque there intervened the typically Italian extravaganza of Mannerism with its inventiveness and its indulgence of the bizarre. In the eighteenth century a change of outlook and taste brought about a change of style, especially in interior decoration, towards the frothy arabesques and mirrored airiness of the Rococo. In Italy the change did not lead to any great employment or development of stone-carving nor was the style anything like as popular as in France and Germany.

The variety of stones and styles in the stonework of succeeding ages in Italy, examples of which are reproduced here, is to be found in all parts of the country – in the small hill-towns of Umbria and the Alps or in the villages of Lazio and Lucania as well as the major cities like Rome, Venice and Florence. The accompanying photographs show some of this variety: Romanesque stonework on the entrance to the cathedral of

ABOVE: *Mourning family in the Staglieno Cemetery near Genoa, which is a vast museum of nineteenth- and twentieth-century sepulchral sculpture in a variety of imitative styles.*

LEFT: *Some of the rich Genoese merchant families commissioned tombs in the Staglieno Cemetery which were as big as houses, and many contain lifesize statues.*

Foligno in Umbria; Gothic stonework from the cathedral of Orvieto and the monastery of San Martino in Naples; Renaissance stone carving from Spello in Umbria, from Lucca and Montepulciano in Tuscany and from the church of San Zaccaria in Venice. There is also the architectural extravaganza of the Casa Longobarda in Asolo. There is an example of Baroque stonework from a fountain in the gardens of the Royal Palace of Caserta. Cemeteries are great museums of nineteenth- and twentieth-century stone-carving and one of the most remarkable of these is the assembly of tombs in the Staglieno Cemetery of Genoa, executed in a wide range of revivalist styles. The inspiration is not of the highest but the technical skill of the sculptors is outstanding. And so it has remained in Italy to this day, although modern building materials and techniques are not generally favourable to the use of stone or the widespread practice and perfecting of stone-carving. The demand for stonework is probably also in decline in our age due to its cost.

MOSAICS

The history of mosaics in Italy is very ancient. In common with much of Italian art, mosaics in Italy are derived from Greek prototypes, although Egyptian mosaic work was also an early and continuing influence. The Greek models were developed rapidly throughout the Hellenistic period in many of the houses of wealthy Romans, as we see in some outstanding examples in Pompeii and Herculaneum. Particularly striking among these is the mosaic (late second century BC), now in the National Art Museum of Naples, representing the defeat by Alexander the Great of the Persian King Darius III in the battle of Issus in 333 BC. It was made in Alexandria of Egypt from a much earlier Greek painting. Mosaic work of this kind composed of many cut cubes of marbles or glass was known as *opus vermiculatum*. Another form of mosaics for pavements, which became very popular throughout the Roman Empire, was called *opus tesselatum*, and was composed of larger black and white stone or marble cubes.

Many of the later pavements at the end of the Republican period, like that of a huge and threatening watchdog in the house of Publius Paquinus Proculus (late second century BC) in Pompeii, were in black and white marble *tesserae* (the small marble or glass fragments of which a mosaic was composed). But quite frequently within the area of the black and white stone or marble design there would be inserted a multi-coloured mosaic picture known as an *emblema*, portraying fish and animals, scenes from mythology and a variety of other subjects. These especially fine mosaics were of the

LEFT: *The Sala del Re Ruggero (King Roger II) in the royal apartments of the Palazzo dei Normanni, Palermo, Sicily, contains twelfth-century mosaics depicting animals (real and mythical) and hunting scenes.*

RIGHT: *Swans in a mosaic on the upper wall of the Sala del Re Ruggero, Palazzo dei Normanni, Palermo.*

opus vermiculatum type.

Under the Empire, the use of mosaics greatly increased. Moreover, at this time mosaics called *opus musivum* began to be applied to walls of Italian houses, together with multi-coloured slabs of marble revetment (*opus sectile*) forming geometric patterns. A fine example of a wall mosaic with glass tesserae is that of Neptune and Amphitrite (see p.42) in the dining room of the house of that name in Herculaneum. The application of mosaic work to walls, and later to vaults, was made possible by the Roman invention of a new cement called *cocciopesto*, made of the water-resistant sand, pozzolana, mixed with powdered marble or lime, in which any desired pattern of fragmented stone could be inserted to form a decoration. Wall mosaics were also ideally suited to the requirements of Christian churches.

With the ending of the persecution of the Christian Church in Constantine's reign, from AD 313 onwards, many Roman mosaic workers employed their skills in the new churches being built in Rome, and splendid examples are to be found in the churches of Santa Costanza (early fourth century), Santa Pudenziana (late fourth century) and the great basilica of Santa Maria Maggiore (mid-fifth century). The development of Constantinople after 330 reached its zenith under

the Emperor Justinian who introduced two dominant strains of mosaic art, an Eastern decorative approach and an intense religious feeling. These qualities emerge concurrently with the Roman tradition of mosaic manufacture in some of the great churches in Ravenna, like Sant' Apollinare in Classe (consecrated 549), where the magnificent mosaic of the apse representing the Transfiguration of Christ on Mount Tabor displays an Eastern symbolism in most of the faces and figures but a classical influence in the glorious depiction of the greensward in the background, with its rocks and trees and flowers, and in its vivid colouring.

Ceiling mosaic depicting the Transfiguration of Christ in the apse of the sixth-century church of Sant 'Apollinare in Classe near Ravenna.

It may be convenient to enumerate briefly some of the distinguishing features of Byzantine mosaic decoration, which was of course almost entirely religious. The most important figure, that of Christ, is usually much the largest and is placed at the top of the picture in the apse or dome of the church. The second largest figure is that of the Virgin Mary, often placed in the conch of the apse. Of lesser figures, the Evangelists tend to occupy the pendentives while Apostles, Fathers of the Church and saints are mostly relegated to subsidiary wall spaces. The Byzantine Christ is bearded and hieratic; the Roman Christ has a youthful, chubby appearance and a beardless face.

The widespread use of gold *tesserae*, especially for backgrounds, is another feature of Byzantine mosaics.

Since there occurred waves of Byzantine immigration into Italy at various times, the element of Byzantine craftsmen who settled in the country remained strong. In the seventh century there was an influx into Italy of Byzantine refugees from Muslim-occupied territories in Palestine and Asia Minor, and at that time cultural links between Rome and Byzantium were strong. In the following century when these links were shattered, other waves of Byzantine immigrants sought refuge in Italy, mostly in the Greek-speaking areas of southern Italy and Sicily. This was the result of the iconoclastic policy of the Eastern Emperor Leo III, who in 726 forbad the veneration of images.

That the Byzantine tradition of mosaic art had a strong and lasting influence in Italy can be seen

Mosaic work on one side of the pulpit by Nicola di Bartolomeo da Foggia in the cathedral at Ravello. This masterpiece of Cosmatesque decoration dates from 1272.

in the great cathedral of St Mark in Venice, where it found an exuberant outlet from the twelfth century onward. Here the elaborate iconography which governs the complex expanse of mosaic work covering nearly every available surface throughout the vast building is essentially Byzantine, with Christ Pantocrator portrayed on his throne in the apse; the Ascension in the central cupola; Pentecost, and the Apostles preaching the Gospel to all men, in the cupola above the nave where the congregation assembled; and the Prophets in the cupola above the high altar. The brilliant reflection of the subdued light within the building is given maximum effect by the skill of the mosaic workers in placing their *tesserae* at different angles to the mosaic bed to achieve the brightest radiance.

In the far south in Apulia, which was governed from Byzantium during two periods (535–53 and 880–1059), we find surprisingly little mosaic work reflecting Byzantine influence. Nevertheless, many mosaic workers entered Italy from Greece through Apulia, so that when the Normans arrived there and established the Duchy of Apulia (1059), they found a skilled workforce of artisans awaiting employment. And during this period under the leadership of a great abbot, Desiderius, the abbey of Monte Cassino became a haven for

Byzantine mosaic artists, who were given charge of most of the church's interior redecoration (*c.*1071).

It was in the twelfth century, after the Norman conquest of Sicily was completed, that the great opportunity for the Byzantine mosaic workers arose. We have already noted how the Norman kings of Sicily became enlightened patrons of the arts, employing the best artists they could attract to their court whether they came from Byzantium, Lombardy or from Muslim North Africa. Among the notable buildings erected or embellished during the reign of King Roger II was the Capella Palatina of the Palazzo dei Normanni in Palermo, where the Byzantine mosaics date from 1140–50. Of the same reign was the cathedral of Cefalù (*c.*1148) with outstanding Byzantine mosaics.

King William II (1154–66), Roger's successor, built the even more opulent cathedral of Monreale, near Palermo, where the Byzantine

Mosaic decoration sparkles on columns in the twelfth-century cloister of the Benedictine monastery attached to the cathedral of Monreale, Sicily.

San Frediano, Lucca, was consecrated in 1147 but the upper elevation of the façade, decorated with a Byzantine-style mosaic, was added in the thirteenth century.

mosaics were finished in 1172. Another style of mosaic is to be found in the extremely beautiful twelfth-century cloister of the Benedictine convent adjoining Monreale Cathedral, where pointed arches are sustained by twin columns of varied shapes, many of which are encrusted with mosaic patterns, as in the work of the Roman Cosmati families who flourished between 1100 and 1300. The marble and mosaic inlay work described as Cosmatesque was itself derived in part from Byzantine models. It is to be found in the pulpit of the cathedral of Ravello (1272) and in many parts of Italy and abroad, as in the chapel of Edward the Confessor in Westminster Abbey and the sanctuary pavement (1268).

Mosaic decoration continued to be employed in Italy. A striking example is a very large mosaic on the fine façade of the Romanesque church of San Frediano in Lucca, and on the front of the Gothic cathedral of Orvieto there are large mosaics from the first half of the fourteenth century. In St Peter's the huge mosaic figures of the Evangelists in the cupola pendentives were designed by comparatively little-known artists of the sixteenth century. From then on, through the succeeding centuries, a series of large copies of paintings, some by well-known painters like Poussin, Guido Reni and Guercino and others by artists of much lesser fame, have been erected in mosaic form on many of the altars of the church. They are tolerable as skilful imitations, and an aid to devotion, but, as one critic said, they barely qualify as works of art. Nevertheless, the tradition of mosaic-making is more active in Italy than elsewhere, and when a mosaic is required in some church abroad, it is probable that Italian artists will be called in to compose and construct it.

Mosaics over a side door of Orvieto Cathedral, representing the Baptism of Christ and designed by Cesare Nebbia (1536–1614). It took nearly 100 mosaic artists several centuries to complete all the mosaics on this facade.

VISITOR'S GUIDE

ABOVE: *A pleasantly shaded entrance surrounded by plants, in the courtyard of the Castello di Decima, Latium.*

LEFT: *The sixteenth-century Baroque façade of one of the palaces in Varallo, Piedmont, a small town well-known as a pilgrimage centre.*

PLACES TO VISIT

*T*he most detailed guides of the Italian provinces (including the main towns) are those of the CTI, the Italian Tourist Club. The guide for Rome in this series is generally acclaimed as the most complete guidebook of the city. Another very useful series is the collection of Blue Guides which includes volumes on northern Italy from the Alps to Rome and on southern Italy from Rome to Calabria. There are separate guides for Sicily and some of the major Italian towns, including Rome, in this series. The excellent Companion Guides to Rome, Florence and Venice published by Collins are referred to separately in the bibliography.

ALBEROBELLO
Trulli

AMALFI
Cathedral (Sant' Andrea)
Chiostro del Paradiso

AREZZO
Piazza Grande
Pieve di Santa Maria
San Francesco (frescoes by Piero della Francesca)

ASCOLI PICENO
Piazza del Popolo

ASOLO

ASSISI
Basilica di San Francesco
Rocca Maggiore (medieval castle)

Santa Chiara

BOLOGNA
Piazza Maggiore and Piazza del Nettuno with the
 Fontana del Nettuno
Leaning Towers (Piazza di Porta Ravegnana)
Pinacoteca Nazionale (gallery)
San Domenico
San Giacomo Maggiore
San Petronio

CAPRI

CASERTA
Royal Palace: gardens

DOLOMITES

FLORENCE
Baptistery
Boboli Gardens
Campanile

ABOVE: *Medieval towers overlooking the main square, the Piazza Grande, in Arezzo, Tuscany.*

Cathedral (Santa Maria del Fiore)
Galleria degli Uffizi
Loggia della Signoria
Museo di San Marco (Fra Angelico frescoes)
Museo Nazionale del Bargello
Ospedale degli Innocenti
Palazzo Medici-Riccardi
Palazzo Pitti (museum and gallery)
Palazzo Strozzi
Palazzo Vecchio
Piazza della Signoria
San Lorenzo
San Miniato al Monte
Santa Croce
Santa Maria del Carmine
Santa Maria Novella

GARGANO PENINSULA
Umbra Forests
Monte Sant'Angelo

GENOA
Cathedral (San Lorenzo)
Piazza San Matteo
Staglieno Cemetery
Via Garibaldi – street of palaces and galleries

GUBBIO
Città Vecchia
Palazzo dei Consoli

HERCULANEUM/ERCOLANO (excavated Roman
    city)

LAKE DISTRICT
Lake Como
Lake Garda
Lake Maggiore (Borromean Islands: Isola Bella)

L'AQUILA
San Bernardino
Santa Maria di Collemaggio

LECCE
Basilica di Santa Croce
Piazza del Duomo
San Matteo
San Giovanni Battista/Rosario

LUCCA
Cathedral (San Martino)
San Frediano
San Michele

MANTUA
Palazzo del Tè

Palazzo Ducale
Piazza delle Erbe

MARTINA FRANCA
Piazza Plebiscito
San Martino

MILAN
Castello Sforzesco
Cathedral
Museo Poldi Pezzoli
Palazzo dell' Ambrosiana (17th-century library)
Pinacoteca di Brera (gallery)
Sant' Ambrogio
Santa Maria delle Grazie

MONTEPULCIANO
Madonna di San Biagio
Piazza Grande
San Agostino

MORTOLA INFERIORE
Hanbury Gardens

NAPLES
Castel Nuovo
Certosa di San Martino (Carthusian monastery)
Museo Archeologico Nazionale
Palazzo e Galleria Nazionale di Capodimonte
Port of Santa Lucia
Teatro San Carlo (opera house)

ORVIETO
Cathedral

PADUA
Basilica di Sant' Antonio
Cappella degli Scrovegni (frescoes by Giotto)
Prato della Valle

PAESTUM (Greek temples)

RIGHT: *View over Florence looking west down the River Arno with the Ponte Vecchia in the centre.*

PARMA
Baptistery
Cathedral
Palazzo della Pilotta (gallery, museum and Teatro
 Farnese)
San Giovanni Evangelista
nearby: Torrechiara (15th-century fortress)

PAVIA
Certosa di Pavia (Carthusian monastery)

PERUGIA
Fontana Maggiore
Galleria Nazionale dell' Umbria
Museo Archeologico Nazionale dell' Umbria
Oratorio di San Bernardino
San Pietro

PISA
Baptistery
Camposanto (cemetery)
Cathedral
Leaning Tower or Campanile
Museo dell' Opera del Duomo (cathedral
 museum)
Santa Maria della Spina

PISTOIA
Piazza del Duomo
Sant' Andrea

POMPEII

PORTOFINO

RAVELLO
Cathedral
Villa Cimbrone
Villa Rufolo

RAVENNA
Mausoleo di Galla Placidia
San Vitale
nearby: Sant' Apollinare in Classe

ROME
Castel Sant' Angelo
Colosseum
Fontana di Trevi
Palatine Hill
Palazzo Barberini (gallery)
Palazzo Doria Pamphili (gallery)
Pantheon
Piazza del Campidoglio and the Musei Capitolini
Piazza di Spagna and the Spanish Steps
Piazza Navona and Fontana dei Fiumi
Roman Forum
St Peter's and the Vatican (Museums)
San Carlo alle Quattro Fontane
San Clemente
San Giovanni in Laterano (cathedral)
San Paolo fuori le Mura
Sant' Andrea al Quirinale
Santa Maria del Popolo

Santa Maria della Vittoria
Santa Maria Maggiore
Villa Giulia (Museo Nazionale Etrusco)

SAN GIMIGNANO
Collegiata (church with frescoes)
Piazza del Duomo
Sant' Agostino

SIENA
Cathedral
Museo dell' Opera del Duomo (cathedral
 museum)
Palazzo Buonsignori/Pinacoteca Nazionale
 (gallery)
Palazzo Pubblico (town hall) and Museo Civico
Piazza delle Campo

SPOLETO
Cathedral
Ponte del Torri
San Salvatore
Sant' Eufemia

RIGHT: *The Ponte and the Castel Sant' Angelo, Rome.*

LEFT: *Part of the Maritime Theatre in Hadrian's Villa (AD 124–135) near Tivoli. Here, in a cluster of beautiful rooms set on an island surrounded by a canal and a portico, the emperor could achieve perfect privacy.*

TIVOLI
Hadrian's Villa
Villa d'Este

TRIESTE
Castello di Miramare
Piazza dell' Unita d'Italia
San Giusto (basilica and castle)

TURIN
Basilica di Superga
Cathedral of San Giovanni (houses the Turin
  shroud)
Galleria Sabauda
Mole Antonelliana
Museo Egizio
Palazzo Madama
Piazza San Carlo
San Lorenzo

URBINO
Palazzo Ducale

VENICE
Accademia (gallery)
Bridge of Sighs
Ca' d' Oro
Doge's Palace
Grand Canal
Libreria Sansoviniana
Palazzo Corner-Spinelli
Palazzo Grassi
Palazzo Rezzonico
Palazzo Vendramin-Calergi
Procuratie (Law Courts)
Rialto Bridge
St Mark's Basilica
St Mark's Square
San Giorgio Maggiore
San Zaccaria
Santa Maria della Salute
Scuola di San Rocco

VERONA
Arche Scaligere (tombs of the Scaligeri)
Castelvecchio e Ponte Scaligero
Piazza dei Signori
Piazza delle Erbe
Roman Arena
San Zeno Maggiore

VESUVIUS
VICENZA
Piazza dei Signori and the Basilica (by Palladio)

Santa Corona
Teatro Olimpico
nearby: Villa Rotonda, Villa Valmarana

near VITERBO
Parco dei Mostri, Villa Orsini, Bomarzo
Villa Lante in Bagnaia

SICILY

AGRIGENTO
Valle dei Templi (Valley of the Temples)

LIPARI ISLANDS

MONREALE
Cathedral and cloisters

MOUNT ETNA

PALERMO
Catacombe dei Cappucini
Cathedral
La Martorana
Palazzo dei Normanni
Piazza Pretoria
San Cataldo
San Giovanni degli Eremiti

SEGESTA AND SELINUNTE
Greek temples

SYRACUSE
Città Vecchia (old town): Piazza Duomo and
  Fonte Aretusa
Zona Archeologica (Greek theatre, etc.)

TAORMINA
Public gardens
Greek theatre

BIBLIOGRAPHY

A

Arciniegas, Germán, *El Mundo de la Bella Simonetta* Editorial Sudamericana, Buenos Aires, 1962.

Arpino, Giovanni *et al.*, *Piemonte Valle d'Aosta*, Electa Milan, 1968.

B

Biancofiore, Franco *et al.*, *Puglia*, Electa Editrice, Milan, 1966.

Borsook, Eve, *The Companion Guide to Florence*, Collins, London, 1973.

Barzini, Luigi, *The Italians*, Hamish Hamilton, London, 1964.

C

Carcopino, Jérome, *La Vie Quotidienne à Rome*, Hachette, Paris, 1948.

Clarke, Ethne and Raffaello Bencini, *The Gardens of Tuscany*, Weidenfield & Nicolson, London, 1990.

F

Fletcher, Sir Banister, *A History of Architecture*, Batsford, London, 1921.

Franciscis, Alfonso De, *Museo Nazionale di Napoli*, De Agostini, Novara, 1965.

G

Gage, John, *Colour and Culture*, Thames and Hudson, 1993.

Griseri, Andreina, *Jaquerio e il realismo Gotico in Piemonte*, Fratelli Pozzo, Turin, 1966.

Gombrich, E. H., *The Story of Art*, Phaidon Press, London, 1950.

H

Hadermann-Misgrec, Lydia, *Images de Ninfa*, Fondazione Camillo Caetani, Rome, 1986.

Herbert, Zbigniew, *Barbarian in the Garden*, Harvest Books, London, 1986.

Hay, Denis, *The Italian Renaissance*, Cambridge, 1961.

Hale, J. R., ed., *A Concise Encyclopaedia of the Italian Renaissance*, Thames and Hudson, London, 1981.

Hall, James, *A History of the Ideas and Images of Italian Art*, Harper, New York, 1983.

Hibbard, Howard, *Michelangelo*, Allen Lane, London, 1975.

Hibbert, Christopher, *Rome: The Biography of a City*, Viking, London, 1985; *Venice: The Biography of a City*, Grafton Books, London, 1988; *Florence: The Biography of a City*, Viking, London, 1993.

Highet, Gilbert, *Poets in a Landscape*, Penguin Books, Harmondsworth, 1959.

Honour, Hugh, *The Companion Guide to Venice*, Collins, London, 1965.

Howard, Deborah, *The Architectural History of Venice*, Batsford, London, 1987; *Architecture and Patronage in Renaissance Venice*, Yale University Press, New Haven and London, 1975.

K

Kempers, Bram, *Painting, Power and Patronage: The Rise of the Professional Artist in the Italian Renaissance*, Allen Lane, The Penguin Press, London, 1987.

Krautheimer, Richard, *Rome, Profile of a City: 312–1308*, Princeton, 1980.

L

Lees-Milne, James, *Saint Peter's*, Hamish Hamilton, London, 1967; *Roman Mornings*, Collins, London, 1988.

M

McCorquodale, Charles, *The History of Interior Decoration*, Phaidon, Oxford, 1988.

Mannoni, Luciano e Tiziano, *Il Marmo*, SAGEP, Genoa, 1978.

Masson, Georgina, *Italian Gardens*, Thames and Hudson, London, 1961; *The Companion Guide to Rome*, Collins, London, 1965

Mazzotti, Giuseppe, *Ville Venete*, Bestetti, Rome, 1958.

Murray, Peter, *The Architecture of the Italian Renaissance*, Schocken Books, New York, 1986.

Medici, Lorenza De', *The Renaissance of Italian Gardens*, Pavilion, London, 1990.

Moorehead, Alan, *The Villa Diana*, Hamish Hamilton, London, 1951.

N

Nicolini, Toni and Tullio Forni, *I Castelli del Piemonte*, LEA, Rome, 1967.

O

Olson, Roberta, *Italian Renaissance Sculpture*, Thames and Hudson, London, 1992.

Ojetti, Ugo *et al.*, *Il Settecento Italiano* (2 vols), Treves-Treccani-Tumminelli, Milan-Rome, 1932.

P

Pallotino, Massimo, *Art of the Etruscans*, Thames and Hudson, London, 1955.

Piovene, Guido, *Viaggio in Italia*, Mondadori, Milan, 1966; *Italy*, Bestetti, Rome, 1958.

Praz, Mario, *La Filosofia dell' Arredamento*, Longanesi, Rome, 1964.

Procacci, Ugo, *Sinopie e Affreschi*, Cassa di Risparmio, Florence, 1960.

Q

Quest-Ritson, Charles, *The English Garden Abroad*, Viking, London, 1992.

R

Ree, Paul van der with Gerrit Smienk and Clemens Steenbergen, *Italian Villas and Gardens*, Troth, Amsterdam, 1992.

S

Sherman, John, *Mannerism*, Penguin Books, Harmondsworth, 1967.

W

Wilson, Philip, *Brunelleschi*, Scala Institutio Fotografico Editoriale Firenze, 1980

Y

Yarwood, Doreen, *The Architecture of Europe: Vol. 2, The Middle Ages: 650 to 1550*, Batsford, London, 1992.

RIGHT: *The main courtyard of the Castello di Decima, an elegant restoration of a medieval castle on the old consular road from Rome to Lavinium, now Pratica di Mare.*

INDEX

Page numbers in *italics* refer to illustrations